Supportive Education

Books are to be returned on or before
the last date below.

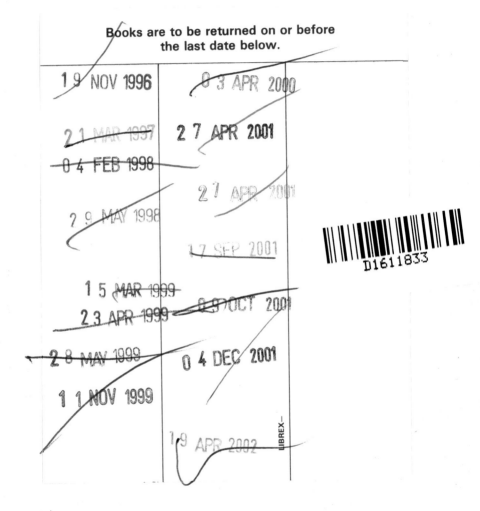

1 9 NOV 1996

0 3 APR 2000

2 1 MAR 1997

2 7 APR 2001

0 4 FEB 1998

2 7 APR 2001

2 9 MAY 1998

1 7 SEP 2001

1 5 MAR 1999

2 3 APR 1999

0 9 OCT 2001

2 8 MAY 1999

0 4 DEC 2001

1 1 NOV 1999

1 9 APR 2002

LIBREX—

D1611833

Supportive Education
An integrated response to pastoral care and special needs

Phil Bell and Ron Best

Basil Blackwell

First published 1986

© Phil Bell and Ron Best 1986

Reprinted 1988

Published by Basil Blackwell Ltd
108 Cowley Road
Oxford OX4 1JF
England

British Library Cataloguing in Publication Data

Bell, Philip
    Supportive education: an integrated response to pastoral care and special needs.
      (Blackwell studies in personal and social education and pastoral care)
    1. School social work   Great Britain
    I. Title II. Best, Ronald E.
    371.4'6   LB3013-4

    ISBN 0-631-14213-4

Typeset in 10 on 11½ Plantin by Multiplex techniques ltd, St Mary Cray, Kent
Printed in Great Britain

To Alan, Colin, Anna, Simon and Peter

Acknowledgements

We would like to acknowledge the contribution and co-operation of Mrs Norma Turner and the staff of The Rickstones School, Witham, Essex. The way in which they have committed themselves to co-ordinating their efforts for the benefit of the pupils has provided much of the inspiration for this book, as well as a model to which other schools would be well advised to give careful consideration.

Thanks are also due to Peter Lang and Peter Ribbins who, as series editors, gave much encouragement and made helpful comments on the manuscript.

Finally, the facilities of the Education Research Centre and library of the Essex Institute of Higher Education are gratefully acknowledged.

Contents

1 Aims and focus

Janet came into the staffroom feeling decidedly irritated. For the second time this week the video had played up while she was trying to show a programme on graphs to 3W4. Heaven knows, as the fourth maths set they were not the easiest class to deal with even when things went right; when the screen went blank the cat calls and comments just had to be heard to be believed. As was so often the case, Jimmy Stephens had been the main culprit, and Janet was not a little pleased with herself for at least not having lost her temper with him again today.

Filling her none-too-clean mug with coffee, Janet wandered across the room to join two of the keep-fit and health-food fanatics who were standing by the notice-board. As usual, they were passing their break-time in deep discussion of aerobics and the relative merits of different activities for keeping a trim figure.

'What do you think Janet?' asked Brenda Allsop. 'Which do you think requires the more energy: squash or badminton?'

'I don't know,' said Janet, 'but I do know I'd like to squash that Jimmy Stephens! He was unbearable again today.'

'You'd be unbearable if you had his problems,' came a voice from across the room.

Janet turned to see Dave Clarkson, the music teacher, peering over the top of the back pages of *The Times Educational Supplement.*

'What do you mean?' she asked.

'Look at the board,' he snapped and disappeared back behind his paper. There on the crowded notice-board she picked out the all too familiar name:

> *To all staff teaching JIMMY STEPHENS, 3W4*
> At the present time this pupil is experiencing personal problems.
> Should you encounter any difficulties with this pupil, please refer
> to Mrs Harris or Mr Spinks.

'How long's that been up there?' she queried.

'Don't know,' said Brenda. 'I hadn't noticed it myself until now, though how one is supposed to notice things amongst this lot, heaven only knows! There are notices here that go back months.'

'Yes,' said Janet crossly, 'including all that stuff to do with last term's concert,' raising her voice and looking hard across the room. There was a snort from behind the *TES*, but the reader was apparently unwilling to be drawn.

'We should really have a memo about that sort of thing,' offered Alison McPhee.

'No memo will get rid of that little brat,' came another voice, this time from Tony Norton, standing by the sink in his usual track-suit with its emblazoned insignia completing his macho image. 'He should have been booted out years ago!'

'Couldn't agree more,' Helen Saunders threw in.

A grunt that sounded like 'Rubbish' came from behind the *TES* and was followed by a ripple of comments from around the now full staff-room.

'Well, I'd better go and find out what it's all about,' said Janet and set off in search of Mrs Harris, the head of Jimmy's house.

She found her in the old stock-room which now served as Mrs Harris's office. She was in conference with John Spinks himself, head of the remedial department and therefore with a better knowledge of Jimmy than most of the staff. They looked up as Janet entered.

'What can I do for you?,' asked Mrs Harris in her usual brisk fashion.

'Hope I'm not interrupting,' Janet began, 'but I saw the notice about Jimmy on the board and thought I'd better come along and find out what it was about.'

'Jimmy who?,' asked Mr Spinks, looking surprised.

'Jimmy Stephens,' said Janet, feeling confused. Surely there was only one notice of *this* kind on the board, and John Spinks's name was clearly on it. Was he being intentionally obtuse?

'I don't know anything about any notice,' he continued, 'but then no one tells me anything around here. I'm just the bloke who gets saddled with everybody's cast-offs.'

'*I* put it up,' said Mrs Harris hurriedly, 'and I was just about to tell you. I've drawn staff's attention to Jimmy as a child with problems. I hope you don't mind, but I added your name as someone else who might provide some insight into his situation.'

'Oh, I see,' said John Spinks, somewhat mollified. 'Well, I *should* be able to. After all, he is a 'remedial' and I have followed his case closely ever since his name cropped up in the first year. The fact is, Janet, that Jimmy has a very serious problem with his comprehension. According to the NFER scores, he had a reading age of 9.6 when he came here from the juniors, which is not all that bad, and he seems able to handle the work I set him, but his other teachers say he can't do even the most simple of comprehension exercises. Though I doubt they're approaching it properly themselves, bearing in mind his lack of ability and the problem at home.'

'Oh,' said Janet, jumping to the obvious conclusion.

'It's not that,' said Mrs Harris. 'I spoke to him only the other day and he says he's *quite* got used to living alone with his dad. The reason he's worrying is because one or two of the kids in his class have been taking the mickey since he started coming to you for extra work, Mr Spinks. Calling him names, for one thing. Perhaps you shouldn't have withdrawn him on such a permanent basis.'

John Spinks began to colour. 'You're not blaming *me*, are you?' he challenged, eyes flashing. 'It's my job to help kids with that sort of problem, but I can't get him to understand what he reads by waving a magic wand! And I certainly can't put his family back together with a snap of the fingers, can I?'

'No one's asking you to,' Mrs Harris retorted. 'Just think a bit more before you whip a kid out of class, that's all!'

'What else am I supposed to do?' he rejoined. 'With only myself and Mrs Reilly in the department, we can't possibly get round to every child in every lesson, so withdrawal is the only answer. Anyway, he wouldn't learn much from some of the people who were teaching him. They just don't know how to teach the basic skills.'

'But can't you see that this is bound to make him conspicuous? It's an invitation to the others to make him the butt of their jokes. I really think you should be more careful in the way you handle the whole withdrawal issue,' Mrs Harris glared at him across the desk.

'And I'd ask you to stick to what you know best and leave the running of the remedial department to me. Come to that, I'd rather you didn't attach my name to notices when the problem's got nowt to do with me. As a matter of fact he wouldn't do *any* comprehension if I didn't withdraw him, because he just won't do anything at all for Helen Saunders. She doesn't like him so he won't work for her. And I don't altogether blame him. To hear her talk, he's hardly human; just some kind of animal who makes her life a misery. She just has no awareness that the kid's got problems, so she stamps on him at every available opportunity. She's as much to blame as anyone, and that's all there is to it!'

'With respect, that's not quite so,' Mrs Harris smarted. 'I sorted all that out by having them both in here for some group guidance. They were smiling at each other when they left. If it ever was a pastoral problem, that's been taken care of.'

'Oh, has it?' John Spinks replied, his tone heavy with sarcasm. 'That's not what Jimmy's father said when I met him in the shops last week! According to him, Jimmy has completely given up doing his English homework, thanks to her sharp tongue. And when I said I thought she wasn't as sympathetic as she might be, he called her a sour old cow.'

'Well, you shouldn't have even mentioned it,' Mrs Harris snapped. 'You are supposed to be a remedial expert not a social worker and you certainly shouldn't criticise your colleagues in public. Perhaps, if you had spent more time talking to Helen Saunders about Jimmy and less time gossiping with his father, this sort of problem might never have arisen.'

By this time Janet was feeling decidedly uncomfortable, and realised that her coffee break had now gone without anything constructive having been achieved. 'If you two can't agree about what's wrong,' she said, turning to go, 'then how am I supposed to know what to do?'

How indeed?

We suspect that many teachers will recognise either the actors or the situation described in this scene. Something like this happens in more than one school every day. Here we have a child – the same child – recognised as having problems for which the school should find a solution. Here we have teachers each, in their own way, trying to find some sort of solution to these problems. Yet the problems they seek to solve and the situation within which those problems are located are perceived very differently by each of them. No doubt Helen Saunders and the others in the staff-room and, indeed, Jimmy himself would provide yet more perspectives on this same 'reality'.

Some progress might have been made, we suppose, had communication between Mrs Harris and Mr Spinks been more frequent and more clear, or if they had at least recognised that the 'problem' was more than one simply of home background, personality clash between teacher and pupil, or peer-group reaction to Jimmy's withdrawal from class for remedial help. Perhaps the confusion might have been reduced had these two teachers had less of a vested interest in protecting their respective empires, defending their attempts to help Jimmy as either a pastoral or a remedial case, and given their efforts to a careful and mutually informative analysis of a shared responsibility. There is little doubt that Janet herself, like Helen Saunders, is in some way to blame for seeing Jimmy not as a child with a problem, but first and foremost as a problem child, a child capable of making a teacher's life a misery by constant disobedience and anti-social behaviour.

We have used this fictitious example to focus attention on what we see as a major concern facing schools: how schools need to be organised and to function so that children like Jimmy – and this may mean *every* child at some point in its school career – receive the kind of support, understanding, and teaching that they need. Not that schools appear unaware of their responsibilities in this direction. Few comprehensives nowadays would admit to having neither a policy nor a structure which could be described as being concerned with 'pastoral care'. Every school will claim to have made some kind of arrangement for the child with particular 'learning problems', whether under the heading of 'remedial education' or some more fashionable euphemism for the education of the 'slow learner'. In the wake of Warnock and the 1981 Education Act, schools are coming under greater and greater pressure to accommodate children with an ever wider range of 'special educational needs'. The implications of these developments for the 'pastoral' as well as the 'academic' support of children have only just begun to bite in most schools.

What is perhaps surprising is the schools' apparent inability to organise these different kinds of support into more integrated, complementary, or at least mutually supportive structures, for, in the final analysis, the remedial and the pastoral have much in common. As Jimmy's case shows, the distinction between, on the one hand, a *personal*, *social* or *emotional* problem (stemming, perhaps, from factors outside the school's control) and, on the other, an *academic* or *learning* problem (originating, or at least emerging, in the child's school experience) is a difficult and possibly false one to draw. Yet 'pastoral', 'academic' and 'remedial' divisions have institutionalised such distinctions in schools up and down the country and, although the motives for so doing may be laudable, there are dangers. The trend to separate and specialise is undeniable. In the last three years, such long-standing professional associations as those of teachers in Science (ASE), English (NATE), and Remedial Education (NARE) have been joined by yet another specialist body: the National Association for Pastoral Care in Education (NAPCE). Such associations do much good work, yet in a way their very existence raises questions about the commitment of schools to the education of the *whole* child, and of *every* child, in which teachers might be expected to unite rather than subdivide. Moreover, both the pastoral and the remedial staff of many schools would claim to be committed to providing the kind of individualised support which children like Jimmy need, yet the support each gives is so often unrelated to what the other is trying to do. This is ironic, since in our experience many of those who have chosen to specialise in pastoral or remedial work are people who are motivated by a concern for the child as a whole *person* whose happiness and general well-being are prized at least as much as, and probably beyond, any notion of simple academic success. It is in their concern for others as *persons* that the best 'remedial' and 'pastoral' staff share a common preoccupation with identifying the *needs* and *problems* of individuals rather than the learning requirements of classes of pupils.

It is the purpose of this book to address the whole issue of how schools may co-ordinate and enhance the provisions they make under the 'remedial' and 'pastoral' labels. We do not presume to be able to provide answers to all the questions we shall raise, nor to be able to make simple and foolproof prescriptions for action. Nor shall we be able to avoid treading on some toes and offending some sensibilities as we attempt to face what is a complex and, in many ways, unsatisfactory reality.

However, we shall be offering some suggestions about the way in which both academic and pastoral support can be better organised and more sensitively provided, and we shall be offering the endeavours of one school which, although inevitably less than perfect, provide a useful model which others might wish to develop. The principles behind these suggestions are those of integration of all kinds of support in meeting the needs of each and every child in the school. To describe this provision we have adopted the label *SUPPORTIVE EDUCATION*. This is not another euphemism for 'remedial' education, teaching the 'slow learner', or the work of the 'special needs' department; nor is it another name for 'pastoral care', or a new slant on 'personal and social education'. Rather, it is a particular way of perceiving the role of the school whereby the divisions and tensions which these different labels create and perpetuate give way to a unified approach to the education of the 'whole' child.

In order to explore the potential of supportive education, we need first to consider what has, to date, been offered in schools. This requires a brief overview of the evolution of 'pastoral' and 'remedial' work in the comprehensive school and a critical analysis of the underlying assumptions of the conventional wisdom. It will also require some consideration of the bureaucratic structures of roles and statuses by which these activities have been institutionalised.

Finally, in bringing together in one book the 'pastoral' and the 'remedial', we hope to provide food for thought for *all* teachers with a genuine interest in the welfare of their children, but we will be concerned primarily with the possibility of supportive education in the *comprehensive* school. In this context we shall have in mind especially those who, like Mrs Harris and Mr Spinks, are in positions of leadership and special responsibility. Teachers, as a rule, don't much like industrial or commercial analogies, but it is important to recognise that schools do have structures in which executive, senior- and middle-management roles may be identified. It is to the senior management of the school and its 'pastoral' and 'remedial' middle managers that this book is especially directed, for it is within their sphere of influence to promote the evaluation, revision and improvement of the organisation and integration in their schools of the various forms which support may take.

2 Remedial education and pastoral care: an overview

The concept of 'needs' is one which features in contemporary discussion and publications about education perhaps as much as any other concept. This is not surprising since education has to do with the fundamental need of the child to grow and develop into a rational, independent and fulfilled adult. As our fictional example in Chapter 1 shows, those needs which are identified with learning and those which are identified with social, emotional and moral adjustment are often difficult to disentangle. We might, therefore, expect the thought and practice of pastoral care in education and the development of ideas and practices designed to deal with learning difficulties of one sort or another to have gone hand in hand.

There are some parallels in the development of these two aspects of school provision, but there seems to have been relatively little interaction between the two. This is, perhaps, because pastoral care as such has only very recently entered the official vocabularies of those involved in education. Thus, Hughes (1980) comments that it is not until the 1974/75 edition of *The Educational System of England and Wales* that pastoral care is even mentioned, sharing a single paragraph with careers and vocational guidance. This does not mean that there is no history of pastoral care in education, but simply that its development has not been carefully chronicled. The same could not be said of developing attitudes to special educational needs, the education of the 'slow learner', and the whole area of meeting needs identified by such concepts as 'backwardness', 'retardation', 'sub-normality' and 'handicap'. The history of such provision is in many ways the history of these concepts and the practices to which they give rise.

From 'different' to 'special need'

Being 'different' is not easy in any society, as anyone from a minority sub-culture will quickly tell you, and to be physically or mentally 'different' can be especially painful. Whether it is the 'animal' in us that makes us fear and turn upon the 'odd one out', the runt in the litter, or the social requirements of the group which requires a scape-goat upon whom to blame everything, it is certainly true that the physically handicapped and mentally abnormal have been the subject of derision and displeasure throughout history (Hewitt,

1974, Pritchard, 1963). Indeed, the plethora of euphemisms which have emerged in order to avoid the stigma of such words as 'cripple' and 'retarded' is itself an indication of the distasteful connotations of such terms.

Ironically, educational progress has been a contributory factor to the growth of such labelling, for it was with the introduction of state education for all in the 1870s that those who for intellectual reasons could not benefit – or at least did not conform – became especially noticeable. After all, in earlier times when relatively few people could read or write, many forms of 'retardation' were simply not open to view, but with the standardised procedures schools adopted for teaching and assessing the three Rs children 'at fault' became 'visible' and were soon recognised as 'problems'. Indeed, there were calls for stern measures with this group, with some worthies encouraging schools to refuse entry to the duller or more troublesome children on the grounds that 'an aggregation of difficult children, urchins who could not be taught (and) ruffians who could not be controlled' would endanger the education of others (Warner, 1890, p134). Moreover, for many of these children 'normal' education was considered unattainable and, as Sir Cyril Burt was to write forty years later, it was believed that 'the majority of backwardness is all round, innate and ineradicable...they must always remain dull, and can never hope to reach the average level' (Burt, 1937, p 606).

By the late 1890s the first special schools and classes were being organised to deal with the most obvious and severe of these educational handicaps, and the Education Act of 1899 required the authorities to make adequate provision for physically and mentally defective children. In time, the category 'defective' was refined and differentiated, with the Act of 1921 widening the brief to include the blind, deaf, epileptic, and the physically and mentally handicapped as requiring separate provision. This gradual development and differentiation of the operative categories went hand in hand with successive pieces of legislation and, of necessity, with the development of offices concerned to discharge these new responsibilities.

The work of Burt (1937) and Schonell (1942) not only established more firmly the notions of ability and measurement according to some concept of the 'normal', but also contributed to the augmenting of local authority bureaucracies with posts created to coordinate action in the areas of both special and remedial provision.

The adoption of a methodology aimed at identifying the 'handicapped' encouraged the growth of special schools, thereby allowing responsibility for the education of such children to pass from the ordinary school teacher into the hands of the recognised expert in the special school. Included under the umbrella term of 'handicap' was Burt's (1952) 'innately dull' group of children whose 'inborn general capacity often inherited from one or both the parents' excluded them from the ordinary school. Into this category fell the 'defective', the 'dull', and the 'backward' and it was suggested that provision for this group should be 'planned and carried out as an organised whole' (Burt, 1952, p15). This recommendation came into force with the 1944 Education Act which introduced the category of handicap known as 'educationally sub-normal' (ESN), an all-embracing term which included a large group who were formally termed 'educable defectives', the 'innately dull' and the 'merely backward'. However before the introduction of this grouping, a compromise had to be made between children identified as 'educationally sub-normal' and the amount of accommodation Burt found at his disposal in London of the 1920s. As a result of the constraints of educational accommodation, it was not possible for all these children to be catered for in a special environment. Ordinary schools, therefore, had to accept a percentage of children who were, by test predictions or definition, borderline ESN (Gipps and Goldstein, 1984).

Even after the introduction of the Act, places for those designated as ESN were limited, and as a consequence ordinary schools began to develop their own organisations to deal with the problem. Schools also had to be content with a growing number of pupils who were failing to benefit from the basics of reading, spelling and number which dominated the curriculum being offered, but who were not sufficiently 'serious' as to warrant ESN status. It was this group – those who were failing educationally, but 'normal' in 'ability', the 'underfunctioning' – who came to be known as 'the remedial group' on the assumption that their educational retardation could be 'remedied' by 'remedial' teaching (Sampson, 1975). In reality, to do poorly in certain subjects for whatever reason involved relegation to the 'bottom' stream and thus the 'remedial group' was also the repository for those who were seen simply as 'of low ability'.

Later developments

In the decade following 1944 there was to be an outcry over the level of the nation's literacy and numeracy skills, and a re-emphasis on the importance of these two areas, which were seen as being the necessary prerequisites for participation in the whole school curriculum. Moreover, children leaving school without having achieved the accepted standards in these skills were considered failures. This necessitated a further increase in the attention given to this aspect of the system, and thus fuelled the movement for 'remedial' education in the ordinary school.

Since then, this concern has surfaced in the context of a variety of research reports and official reviews often entailing a wide range of categories whose precise relations to each other remain a source of mystification to the uninitiated. The Newsom Report (1963) made a plea for the fifty per cent of pupils who fell into the category of those with 'average and below average ability', calling for a change of 'environment...curriculum...and educational approach', (p87, para 264) but in the process confirming the existing view that one could work from a premise of ability as both definable and measurable. A report by the DES (1971) accepted the concept of 'slow learners', and then made the disturbing announcement that some secondary schools were struggling to cope with the fact that from twenty to sixty per cent of their pupils might not achieve what was, by conventional standards, academic success. Such a figure would account for the judgements of those who, like Westwood (1975), could describe some secondary schools as being 'grave-yards of human potential' (p157) when it came to the child with learning problems. Although the figures are rather less dramatic – more like fifteen per cent – the reports of Bullock (1975), Clark (1979) and Rutter et al (1979) have all highlighted the problems of pupils with learning difficulties, especially in the area of reading.

But it is the Warnock Report (1978) which has proved the most significant development in the field since 1944, seeking to replace prevailing categories of handicap with that of 'Special Educational Need', and identifying as many as twenty per cent of children as falling into this category by virtue of learning difficulties of one sort or another. More importantly, the report laid the foundations for the 1981 Education Act which purports to present a new deal for such children through, amongst other things, their greater integration within the ordinary school.

Structures and institutions

The nature of the institutions in which 'different' children should receive an education has, of course, been an issue for a great many years, and the diversity of arrangements which exist and have existed is considerable.

Ordinary schools have answered the call to make provision for children with special needs usually by innovation within their existing bureaucracies. A cursory glance at *The Times Educational Supplement*, reveals the variety of titles and structures which are now emerging, but in the past these have most often been reduced to creating a 'department' and a head of department who decides the curriculum and teaching policy, usually working with one or two full-time assistant teachers to discharge these responsibilities across the years. Though some talk of 'remedial empires' might be permissible in large schools where size has necessitated a net so large for traditional 'remedial children' as to absorb the responsibility for those who are 'backward' because of 'social and cultural limitation', 'lowish ability' and 'emotional difficulties', the 'remedial' department has more often been a relatively small unit.

It has also (as the National Association for Remedial Education often points out) tended to lack status and has all too often had to struggle in the face of inadequate resourcing. The picture of the 'remedial teacher' and his flock living a hermit-like existence in a hut, both socially and geographically isolated from the mainstream of school activity (see Best, 1985) might not now be true of most schools, but it is not far from the truth in some. In this regard, the widening of the 'special needs' net has come as a breath of fresh air to some remedial departments, implying, as it does, a change in the relationship between the department and the rest of the school, and carrying with it an increased status. The teachers are no longer 'remedial' – seen as akin to their pupils in more ways than is publicly acknowledged – but are seen as having special skills and expertise which are necessary to meet the learning needs of 'special' children, rather than merely having the ability to handle, manage or control (rather than educate) the more awkward and troublesome elements in the school (Widlake, 1975).

Whether or not such children should be educated in 'ordinary' rather than 'special' schools is, of course, a debate of long standing and one complicated by the great diversity of arrangements existing in different authorities. Whilst Green (1969, p9) could argue that, so far as academic standards and social competence were concerned, there was little significant difference between the performance of the two, Brennan (1971) could foresee problems in a situation where a child's educational future was completely at the mercy of fortuitous local circumstances. Whatever the opposition, there was a growing belief among educationalists that the handicapped or disadvantaged should be educated in normal rather than special schools, a belief finally endorsed by the Government in 1981.

Special schools have, of course, developed and differentiated since 1944 and by and large have developed their own curriculum. Educationalists whose interests span the range from 'severe disability' to 'the slow to learn' (Brennan, 1978; Gulliford, 1971) have been concerned to make recommendations in regard to the offerings these schools make, and local authority advisers with responsibility for special education have made a considerable contribution. It is arguable, therefore, that guide-lines on content and method exist for special schools while provision in ordinary schools has been somewhat adrift and lacking any authoritative source. Pragmatism and eclecticism in the face of local circumstances have often been the order of the day.

Local authority services and in-service training

Concurrent with the expansion of special schools and remedial education in the ordinary school came the rise of increased services at local authority level. Advisory teachers were appointed to monitor, advise and occasionally teach those children with particular handicaps. Some authorities have developed their advisory service to include teams of peripatetic remedial teachers who are sent out like 'hit squads' into specific trouble-spots or roam the countryside, breaking their journeys with short stays in schools to examine/test those children giving concern to the school. Where the results reveal uncertainties that the advisory team feel unable to cope with, the help of the school's psychological services may be enlisted. In some authorities, these two agencies combine to provide screening procedures for the early identification of children with needs. A variety of additional support services has also grown up, and Gulliford (1971) is amongst those who have recommended the close integration of the school psychological service with other specialist help to enable accurate diagnoses to be made. Child-guidance centres, special tutorial units, and intermediate treatment centres have been a natural progression and addition to the system. Schools often seem very willing to pass on their problems to higher authorities who are recognised as having expertise to deal with the child's particular problem, with the result that these institutions now strain under the weight of demand for their services.

Finally, there is the inspectorate itself, where there is usually at least one person responsible for special education. However, as 'one-man bands', those chosen for this senior position have frequently had to work hard to meet the needs of the schools and teachers they serve. Their role has included involvement in the appointment of heads of remedial departments or similar middle and senior management positions in the special schools, the organisation and management of both local authority and DES courses covering aspects of the education of children with 'problems' of varying severity, advising the education officer, education committee and other interested parties on matters associated with special needs provision and the general inspection of the schools and departments under their jurisdiction.

While it is desirable that these services should be closely linked to provide regular reviews of the children with whom they are involved, in many instances the demands on the time for each respective service make such interchange and liaison extremely patchy.

Whilst this development has been taking place, teachers' centres, colleges and institutes of education have devised courses of in-service training, ranging from one-day conferences to year-long full-time award-bearing courses, aimed at satisfying the need for suitably qualified personnel for both special and ordinary schools. Unfortunately, the cuts in educational expenditure have in recent years led to a drastic reduction in full-time teacher secondments, and special needs teaching has not always been seen as a priority for those few secondments that have been available.

Public provision for staff development has, of course, been supplemented by the activities of the teachers' own professional body, the National Association for Remedial Education (NARE). For the last twenty years the Association has published its own journal, *Remedial Education*. However, in line with current trends, February 1986 saw the launch of its successor, *Support For Learning*. NARE provides both local and national discussion groups, conferences and publications to encourage discussion and give advice on resources, teaching materials, curriculum development and evaluation, and on the assessment and treatment of specific learning disabilities (Widlake, 1975).

Pastoral care and remedial education

All these developments are clearly to do with making provision for children who are, for any of a variety of reasons, 'special' in respect of their capacity for learning. The long-standing concern with these needs and the fact that the discipline which has almost exclusively informed the evolving concepts and practices has been psychological is an expression of the commitment of schooling to cognitive pursuits first and foremost. In a way, the relative neglect, at least in the literature, of children's needs as persons rather than pupils is a further expression of this preoccupation. Yet there is a sense in which schools as pastoral organisations with a commitment to the child as more than an empty vessel to be filled with knowledge go back a very long way indeed.

In their discussion of the growth of pastoral care Ribbins and Best (1985) use the chronologies of Lang (1983) and Blackburn (1983) to divide the growth of pastoral care into five phases. The first of these (which they call the 'pre-history' of pastoral care) pre-dates the use of the term itself. According to Lang (1982), the ideological roots of pastoral care can be seen in the work of public school reformers from the late eighteenth century onwards. Arnold of Rugby is the popular example, but he was by no means the only nor even the first headmaster to be so motivated. Interestingly, 'religious and moral principles' and 'gentlemanly conduct' took precedence over 'intellectual ability' in pursuing the Christian ideal with his charges. Much of the competitive, sporting ethos and the concept of house loyalty and house spirit in comprehensive schools can be traced back to those early ideals and to the dogma of the 'muscular Christian' which emerged from them.

As in the case of remedial education, the entry of the state into educational provision in 1870 was a significant influence on attitudes to the pastoral needs of the child. In contrast to the public school tradition, elementary schools seemed to have seen their pupils as in need of careful control and socialisation lest the 'lower orders' became a challenge to order (Simon, 1960). There seems also to have been a missionary mentality which combined 'moral earnestness' with smug condescension towards the working classes which perhaps concealed what was really a strengthening of social control. As Ribbins and Best (1985) summarise:

> 'In effect, this pre-history was characterised by the dogma of the
> Christian 'ideal', only there were, it seems, TWO ideals: one, the
> man who would be fit to administer realm, Empire and industry;
> the other, the man who would obediently and diligently labour
> in and consume the products of that industry'.

In the late 1940s the extension of systematic state provision of secondary education was accompanied by the institutionalisation of structures identified with pastoral care. With comprehensive reorganisation, the variety and complexity of vertical, horizontal, and matrix systems increased, and by the late 1960s no self-respecting comprehensive school would have been without one. Ribbins and Best's (1982) third stage of thinking about pastoral care is, in fact, the period in which what has been described as a 'conventional wisdom' was developed to describe and justify the existence and practices of these structures. Books by Marland (1974), Blackburn (1975) and Haigh (1975) provided practitioner-based justifications and analyses of pastoral care in schools, while academics (Craft and Lytton, 1969, and Moore, 1970) researched and theorised about pastoral care as a response to the growing size of schools, the changing nature of children, and the pressures of a society in transition.

Best *et al* (1983) have summarised this wisdom as follows:

'First, "pastoral care" is seen as a *central task* for the school, an integral part of the educational provision for which schools exist. It is no longer possible, if it ever were, to imagine a secondary school can discharge its obligations to its children through instruction in subject matter alone. Teachers recognise the need to create warm, convivial institutions within which the individual child can feel secure, and from which he can draw help and support in resolving a variety of problems – emotional, inter-personal, academic and so on – which his experience both in and out of school present.

Second, "pastoral care" is held to be something which cannot be left to chance. If you want pastoral care to "happen", then you have to institutionalise it. In schools this has meant the design and implementation of separate bureaucratic structures of roles and institutions – the "pastoral system" of "Houses", "Years", etc, – in which role-incumbents are identified as having a more or less specific or general responsibility for the welfare of specific groups of children. Through these arrangements, children can be helped to answer fundamental questions about their own identity and their own path through life.

Third, the existence of pastoral-care systems as we know them is perceived as a relatively recent innovation, roughly coincidental with the reorganisation of secondary schools along comprehensive lines.

We find, in the "conventional wisdom", explanations of this innovation at a number of levels. At the grass roots, teachers are more prepared to see themselves as more than merely imparters of knowledge, and their willingness to be committed to the interests of children as people, as well as pupils, finds a natural expression in the pastoral dimensions of their roles. For head teachers and educational planners, the advent of formal pastoral systems was an institutionalised response to the same kinds of sentiments, but heightened by problems posed for children by the larger educational units being created. Through such systems, comprehensives could be made more meaningful, effective and humane institutions, by a reasoned and realistic policy of specialisation and task-differentiation.

Viewed from the more global perspective of the educational theorists, these changes can be explained as adjustments by the education system to pressing social demands on the one hand, and to changing political and educational philosophies on the other. The needs of a technological society in process of rapid change both impose demands for new sorts of "educated men", and create problems of pupil choice and flexibility. Accompanying changes in attitude to the concept of education, and the liberal-egalitarian emphasis on equality of opportunity and the desirability of a plurality of values, both exacerbated these problems and brought to light others, in particular the problems of providing an educational system which met the demands of both economic efficiency and social justice.' (pp 20-21).

According to Lang (1983) the late 1970s saw the emergence of two parallel developments which he calls 'technique' and 'critique'. The first of these he identifies with the growing concern of schools to improve what they do rather than simply react to problems when they arise. The development of schemes like *Active Tutorial Work* and of curricula with a pastoral flavour (e.g. personal and social education) and a concentration on teaching skills in group work, guidance, etc, are examples of this concern. 'Critique' he identifies with a growing body of literature, some of it research-based, which calls into question some of the more bland and conservative justifications for the growth of pastoral care systems. In short, the orthodox view that the reality of pastoral care in schools is concerned with the resolution of children's problems is being challenged by an alternative explanation of pastoral care as solving the problems of teachers as administrators and disciplinarians, and of schools as agents of social control.

Although, as we have pointed out, remedial and other forms of education to do with academic needs and schools' institutionalised pastoral care seem to share a common concern with needs and problems, there are obvious differences in the traditions within which they have evolved. Pastoral care has rarely been perceived as a central concern of the school in the same way as academic needs have been, nor is it informed primarily by the discipline of psychology. Rather, pastoral care has been justified and analysed much more from sociological perspectives.

Concepts, concepts and more concepts

An interesting feature of thought in these two areas has to do with the concepts that are used. Both the literature of remedial education and that of pastoral care is characterised by a range of concepts whose relationship to each other is by no means always clear. What is interesting is that in the area of special needs these concepts relate to the nature of the child's problem whereas in pastoral care the diverse concepts are really to do with the practices of teachers.

This is especially serious since the conventional wisdom holds that both pastoral care and special needs education are child-centred.

This range of concepts in special needs education includes the ideas of the 'remedial' child, the 'slow learner', the 'dull', the 'backward', the 'retarded', the 'sub-normal', the 'physically handicapped', and the 'specific learning disabled'. This array is confusing to anyone approaching the area from the outside and indeed an analysis of the way these terms are used exposes a lack of clarity and shared understandings. For example, the 'slow learner' is sometimes equated with the 'backward' (DES, 1971), sometimes with the 'dull' (Williams, 1970), and sometimes with a mixed bag of 'mildly dull' and/or 'retarded' children (Brennan, 1974, p16). In fact, according to the usage of Brennan (1974) and others a child may be:

> 'backward' because 'dull'
> 'backward' because 'retarded'
> 'backward' because 'dull' and 'retarded'
> 'retarded' without being either 'dull' or 'backward'

or apparently none of these things and therefore 'normal'. How these various conditions are responded to by schools and teachers has given rise to a corresponding range of labels for kinds of education. Thus, Westwood (1975) distinguishes between 'adaptive', 'compensatory', 'remedial', 'therapeutic' and 'special education' while Brennan (1978) prefers 'adaptive developmental', 'corrective' and 'remedial'.

To find one's way through this maze of terminology is perhaps an impossible task. Words are used in very different ways according, in part at least, to the different traditions from which writers come. Those who see themselves as first and foremost teachers in ordinary schools often seem to speak from a perspective quite different from that of the 'specialist' in learning problems. It seems that the choice and definition of terms is undertaken from the position that, 'When I use a word, it means just what I choose it to mean' (McLeod, 1983, p23), which is profound, but quite unhelpful! As Gains (1980) observes, the result is that 'there seem to be as many definitions of the term ('remedial') as there are practitioners', (p7) while Ablewhite (1977) concluded that the concept had become no more than a loose term, 'in danger of meaning nothing at all' (p8). Not surprisingly, confusion remains as to whether 'remedial teaching' means teaching at a slower pace, special teaching, revising and/or putting a greater emphasis on the basics, therapy, training, compensating or purely 'education' (whatever that may mean).

Attempts at stating the *aims* of remedial education have hardly clarified the issue. Most often the aim has been described by reference to some concept of a set norm attainable by all and used as a yardstick for identifying a shortfall in attainment. Gulliford (1971) sees remedial education as 'part-time, relatively short-term, limited to specific objectives... remedying failures or difficulties in learning certain school subjects', (p7) and for Leach and Raybould (1977) children can 'achieve this within their normal environment'. (p119). However, this whole concept is questionable by those who, like McNicholas (1979), consider that 'the goal of raising everyone's standards to a norm is incapable of achievement' (p30).

When the medical analogy is remembered, the focus of the aim alters to the condition itself: the use of words like 'remedy', 'treatment' and so on indicate the degree to which remedial education is seen as aiming to 'put right what is wrong' (Ablewhite, 1977). Even the commendable intentions of the NARE guidelines for remedial education (Gains and McNicholas, 1979, pp 180–189) confirm the notion of a pathological condition when they proclaim the need for the 'prevention, investigation and treatment' of learning difficulties. The implications of the medical analogy are something to which we shall return below.

The gradual blurring of the original distinction between 'remedial' and 'special' education, based on the educational establishment in which it was provided, has, of course, acccompanied developments over the last two decades. Whether 'remedial' is an integral part or sub-category of 'special education' (Westwood, 1975; Brennan, 1974), or whether the two should be synonymous, or whether remedial teaching describes a set of methods and techniques for achieving 'special education', remains a matter for debate.

Pastoral care: concept and process

While pastoral care theory has a set of categories which correspond to those outlined above there is no parallel classification of the conditions of the children for whom the care is to be provided. Thus, the confusion lies in trying to distinguish between pastoral care, counselling, the tutorial function and personal, academic and vocational guidance. Some have attempted to clarify the relationship between such concepts (Best *et al*, 1977) but like the categories of 'special' and 'remedial' education they continue to be used in varying combinations and sometimes interchangeably, while the recipients of care are not classified nor their conditions measured in a way comparable to the 'dull', 'retarded', etc. We shall return to the question of the validity and utility of these kinds of labels in subsequent chapters. Suffice it for the moment to note that they are given concrete reality every time we group children and allocate responsibilities to teachers within schools.

One thing which both special needs and pastoral care have in common is that they are built into the structural organisation of the school. As we have noted above, it is part of the 'conventional wisdom' of pastoral care that vertical systems of houses, horizontal systems of years and variations upon these themes are manifestations of the school's commitment to the total welfare of its children. However, this has almost always been as an adjunct to the main (academic) division of the school into subject departments, related only through a hierarchical structure of head of department posts, and allocation of pupils to classes on the basis of some concept of 'ability'. The organisation of 'remedial' provision must also be seen in this context. Indeed, a school's conception of 'remedial' education and the way in which children and teachers are organised for the 'remedial' endeavour will be part and parcel of this organisation. Where schools stream children on the basis of 'ability' and 'achievement', deduced from a battery of normative tests and/or on previous school reports, the 'remedial' group may simply be the lowest stream, and it is not uncommon to find such a class operated as a full-time unit. Implicit in such an arrangement is the assumption that to be 'bottom' in certain subjects signifies failure in, and the need for 'special' provision for, *all* subjects. So much can depend on 'reading age', 'verbal ability' and 'numeracy', all of which have norms of acceptability.

To avoid this rather rigid system some schools prefer banding, which implies that 'coarser' divisions of year groups can be effective. Band 'A' collects the 'average' and 'above average', placing the remainder, 'below average', in Band 'B'. Here again identification is not a free choice, but governed by standardised test results. Further to this, a distinction may be made allowing for full- or part-time withdrawal of those with 'special' needs.

Of late, the more respectable and acceptable organisation is that of subject setting. Pupils are allocated to a set on the basis of their individual 'abilities' in each particular subject area. In theory classes should disperse and change for each subject, with the original class forming a group only for registration or form periods. In practice the members of the sets tend to be common and remain together for all academic subjects.

What is common to all three patterns or organisations is the view that the child has particular qualities or features – usually thought of as 'ability' – which can be identified and accurately measured in some way. Even 'mixed ability' implies that you can determine abilities in order that they can be mixed.

It is as well to remember, however, that the provision made in ordinary schools is only one part of the picture. In respect of children with one or another sort of handicap, and this can include the milder forms of handicap to which the label 'remedial' is usually applied, the National Bureau for Co-operation in Child Care (1970), cited by Gulliford (1971, p8), published the report, *Living with Handicap*, which identified no less than thirteen different ways in which provision is organised:

1 Full-time residential special schools
2 Hospital schools
3 Residential special schools with provision on a five-day-week basis
4 Residential special schools serving as a base from which pupils attend appropriate ordinary schools in the neighbourhood, full-time or part-time
5 Residential hostels providing tutorial help for pupils attending normal schools full-time
6 Multi-purpose hostels providing for a variety of handicaps and also providing short-stay facilities for handicapped children and relief in family crisis
7 Day special schools

8 Day special schools allowing some pupils to attend neighbouring ordinary schools part-time

9 Special classes in ordinary schools and special units attached to ordinary schools

10 Peripatetic teaching such as remedial teachers and peripatetic teachers of the deaf

11 Resource centres in ordinary schools including bases for materials, equipment, remedial and other specialist teachers

12 Home tuition

13 Full integration in the ordinary school

Although the Warnock Report, (1978) and the 1981 Education Act have led to a concentration on those towards the bottom of this list, attempts at various degrees of integration will inevitably be influenced by what has gone before. It is really a question of how what is to be integrated is perceived, and that perception is based on the assumption made about needs and conditions which underlie the other forms of organisation in the list.

While pastoral care tends to be seen much more exclusively as a 'normal school activity' it must be noted that other forms of provision are also involved. These can range from individual tuition for children with emotional difficulties in group settings, one-to-one counselling, sanctuaries and special units for 'disturbed' but academically 'normal' children, through the activities of home-school liaison teachers, school-based social workers, school medical officers, educational welfare officers and the educational psychology service, to residential schooling for children who are in care or considered to be at risk in some way or other. A recurring theme throughout this book will be the degree to which it is either possible or desirable to provide the necessary pastoral care and academic support for those children who need it within the ordinary school.

3 The conventional wisdom: a critical analysis

In the previous chapter we briefly described some of the historical developments in the thought and practice of both 'remedial education' and 'pastoral care', and attempted to give some kind of picture of the conventional structures and procedures which exist under these headings. Quite early in that discussion, it was made apparent that the development of 'pastoral care' and 'remedial' education had by no means followed the same pattern. Nor were they informed by the same intellectual traditions, one being based essentially upon educational psychology, the other being more sociological in flavour. None the less, we indicated that there was an avowed common concern at the root of both – a concern with meeting the needs of particular ('special') groups of children – and that, if nothing else, these two areas are similar in so far as each is characterised by a set of ill-defined and overlapping concepts, and each is institutionalised structurally within our schools. We also suggested that bound up in all this, there were important assumptions about what it was that constituted 'education', and why some children required some kind of special support which others did not.

In this chapter we shall explore further these and other ideas which seem to be common in thinking about these two expressions of care. We shall suggest that these are *ideological* in character – that is to say, they are not demonstrable as empirical facts, but are more or less clear or unclear ideas which express and reflect a particular set of values in our society – and we will develop some of the critiques of conventional thought and practice that have been advanced by others.

In exploring some of the key assumptions which seem to be involved in the thought and practice of teachers concerned with meeting the pastoral and learning needs of children, we shall note the rhetoric of schools' commitment to education broadly conceived, and the reality which is often a form of 'product teaching' in which the dominance of our academic traditions seems to give the lie to the claims of more progressive elements. We shall suggest that the function of both pastoral care and remedial education is subordinated to the expectations of the mainstream curriculum and that this dominance can be seen in our perception of children's needs as defined by prevailing notions of 'ability' and 'normality'.

We shall see that there is a diversity of 'causes' which have been identified by those concerned with educational failure, and that the resultant categorisation can be very divisive. Teachers (and others concerned to provide a more effective education) are caught in the tension between the need for diagnosis and identification on the one hand, and the dangers of categorisation and labelling on the other. The unintended consequences of this commitment to catering for 'special needs' – pastoral or remedial – is a major theme in this chapter.

Education or schooling?

The writers of school brochures and prospectuses, and those senior members of staff who address parents' evenings (often, it seems, preoccupied with market forces and the need to impress parents of prospective pupils with the merits of their school) are prone to the attractiveness of such clichés as 'the education of the whole child'. Readers and listeners find themselves hearing about the work of the art department, the fine dramatic presentations for which the school is supposedly renowned, the tradition of sports and sportsmanship, and the development of pastoral care and associated subjects like 'Personal and Social Education', 'Life Skills' and 'Health Education'. As a result, they may well be given the impression of a school committed to the all-round development of the child. Yet when it comes to question time, the discussion will quickly turn to examination results, the available combinations of subjects in the option scheme, and even the school's past record in getting youngsters into Oxbridge and the other universities. It is as though lip-service must be paid to an ideology of 'Education-with-a-capital-E' before the prevailing concept of 'education-as-academic-subjects-leading-to-exams-and-all-the-doors-they-open-to-you' takes over. In short, the discussion of education quickly becomes a discussion of *schooling*. Education as an end in itself gives way to schooling as merely an instrumental activity.

Moreover, in the process, the scope of that which counts as 'the curriculum' is rapidly narrowed, for in any open evening, it is the traditional *academic* subjects which become the focus of attention. Parents are not often seen queueing for an hour to see their child's PE teacher, nor is the drama teacher or the art teacher – let alone the 'life skills' teacher – likely to be inundated by questioning parents. Indeed, despite the appearance of some new 'subjects' and some superficial integration of old ones (usually in the early years of schooling or for groups of 'low-status' pupils) the curriculum is not much changed in its fundamentals nor in the relative appeal of its constituents. It remains essentially a 'collection code' (Bernstein, 1971) of subjects strongly distinguished from each other by formal and informal boundaries of one sort or another ('classification' and 'framing', in Bernstein's terms). Within that collection, the relative *status* of subjects has also changed little: what counts is pretty much what counted a hundred or more years ago: those subjects involving literacy and numeracy, pursued individually and competitively rather than collectively and co-operatively, and perceived as 'school knowledge' generally well insulated from the 'common-sense knowledge' of every-day life (M F D Young, 1971).

The prevalence of these values is immediately seen if we look at either 'pastoral care' or 'remedial education'.

Whatever the avowed commitment of schools to the personal, social and emotional adjustment and well-being of their charges – a concern for them as more than 'empty buckets into which knowledge can be poured' (G Haigh, 1975, p2) – a glance at the time-table of just about any comprehensive school is illuminating. If pastoral care appears at all, it will be either an unspoken ingredient of something called a 'tutor period', or else it will appear as a subject with a pastoral flavour such as 'personal development'. If the former, then provision may well stretch across the years, but is unlikely to be much articulated: it is rather more likely to be something which has been introduced in early years, but not followed up, or is so much in the hands of individual tutors lacking know-how, commitment or training (P Maher and R Best, 1985) that it is treated by staff as an 'optional' part of their work. If the latter, then it is almost certainly a restricted offering to particular years (the fourth and fifth) or particular sections (the 'less able') which, due to the time-table demands of 'real' subjects, receives a totally inadequate allocation of time and resources. (The cynical reader may wish to add that there is also a tendency for such work to be time-tabled at inauspicious moments: the 'Friday afternoon syndrome'). As a non-examination subject, all too often it enjoys a relatively low status in the eyes of teachers and pupils alike.

Of course, there are exceptions: schools where inspired leadership and real commitment by key staff (and that does not necessarily mean the head and deputies, although their support will be priceless) can create the environment necessary for such pursuits to be highly valued. Even then, interest is likely to dwindle in the eye of the consumer as the date of public examinations looms larger, or else such pursuits are linked to the development of examinations in which the 'pastoral' ends up being forced to ape its (academic) betters.

Process or product?

It is sad but true that 'pastoral ' subjects lack status unless they are examined, yet lose their essential *caring* character when attempts to enhance their status force them into the traditional examination mould. In effect, the subject is distorted by a move from what Williamson (1980) calls a 'process' model to a 'product' model of teaching in which 'education is approached as the production of a standardised commodity (such that) the raw materials (children) have somehow to be induced to stay on the conveyor belt and accept the practices of the assembly-men (teachers) as legitimate' (p173).

Instead of open-ended, experiential learning through group work, self-assessment, etc, such subjects can quickly become a corpus of 'facts' to be 'bolted on' to children as they pass through our hands, thus losing entirely the dynamic and processual character of personal development.

There is a further sense in which the traditional academic values dictate the form which 'pastoral care' may take, and this may be seen in the 'under-labourer' role which tutorial programmes are seen as performing for the curriculum. Hamblin's 'critical incidents' (1978, p18) are a case in point. Here, the tutorial programme takes its shape from points of potential crisis for the child, arising out of the academic work of the school, and is ultimately about removing personal, social or psychological impediments to subject-learning. Initially, the argument for such a programme was that it eased the personal and emotional problems *resulting* from the child's encountering anxiety in changing school expectations, the need to make difficult choices and to face up to particular traumas (as in encountering option-choices and examination anxieties). However, more recently Hamblin has joined those whose main concern appears to be with study skills (Hamblin, 1981), and although the *pastoral* dimension of the 'service' is still evident, it is, after all, the traditional academic skills of note-taking, summarising, revising, memorising and (dare we say it?) 'swotting' which are involved. Looked at in this way, pastoral care may even be depicted as a means of support for the school as it goes about its task of 'product teaching' in a way quite inimical to the school's avowed commitment to child-centredness (Williamson, 1980, *op cit*, pp 171–3).

The dominance of academic values is equally evident when one considers remedial education. As with 'pastoral care', schools may well pay lip-service to the idea of the 'whole child', yet remedial departments are primarily concerned with a limited range of skills reflecting a narrow (one-dimensional) model of the child. In an attempt to avoid some of the connotations of the word 'remedial', and to escape from the conventional expectations of 'remedial' departments, some schools have adopted the label 'basic skills'. Yet certain 'basic skills' do not seem to be included in their work. One might, for example, consider interpersonal skills – the presentation of one's 'self' to others, oral communication, listening skills, etc, – as the most basic of all, yet they may not figure much in the department's work, or will be secondary to those more traditional skills of academe. Some might argue that there are 'basic skills' in any physical activity – ball-skills in sport or voice-projection in drama and music, for example – and that these ought to be the primary concern of the remedial teacher, but it is not these which take precedence either. If such skills as these *are* basic, there should be nothing odd about the concept of, for example, 'remedial PE' or 'remedial drama', yet teachers simply do not use the concept in this way at all. As Gurney (1976) sums up:

> 'In theory, there is no reason why the "remedial" label should not be attached to any group or service where children are being helped to catch up, though there seems to be something inherently absurd about the idea of "remedial art" or "remedial music". In

practice, "remedial" nearly always implies help with the 3 Rs and often with only 1 R, Reading' (p13).

As in the case of 'pastoral care', 'remedial education' is seen as performing an 'underlabourer' role for the traditional curriculum subjects. While pastoral-care staff remove the personal, emotional and psychological impediments to learning, the remedial department sets about clearing the undergrowth of reading difficulties and the weeds of innumeracy from the field wherein the seeds of geography, history, English, mathematics and science may be sown.

In all this, there is a preoccupation with transforming the child to fit a given curriculum rather than transforming the curriculum to satisfy the needs of the child. Rather than specify the standards of literacy and numeracy expected of children able to participate in 'normal' lessons within any subject, there is a reliance on standardised tests to identify those who will be withdrawn from 'normal' lessons and offered a separate curriculum of special help. How these tests relate to 'abilities' across a variety of subjects is rarely considered.

The pastoral/academic split

It is here, however, that we see the fundamental division between the two expressions of care and support for the child which we know as 'remedial education' and 'pastoral care': the academic and the pastoral. For it is clear that 'remedial' education is *within* the traditional academic concept of schooling, precisely because the skills with which it is concerned *are* skills of literacy and numeracy. The skills with which 'pastoral care' is engaged are of a different order: they are more often seen as *supplementing* or *complementing* the mainstream academic work of the school than as being inherent within it.

Not everyone likes this distinction, of course, and there is now a well-developed argument for the denigration of the 'pastoral/academic split' (see Best and Ribbins, 1983). But denigration does not, on its own, make something disappear – and the fact that schools can create divided systems of pastoral and academic (remedial) support is an indication of the degree to which such a division is entrenched in conventional thought and practice. And within that division it is clear that it is the traditional concept of education as the mastery of knowledge in the academic curriculum which has dominated the educational scene.

Needs and ability

A second key assumption which seems to be presumed by both 'pastoral care' and 'remedial education' relates to the perceptions we have of the clientele for these forms of support. Put bluntly, there is an assumption that there are two groups of children: those who *need* something 'extra' to normal classroom learning and those who don't. Indeed, the concept of 'need' is perhaps the most potent and pervasive idea underpinning both remedial and pastoral provision. Where 'remedial' education is concerned, the identification of a particular group of children as 'in need' is a prerequisite – and justification – for their being singled out for special educational treatment which is assumed to be beneficial because it is provided by someone who is at least designated as having a specialist role in this area. Teachers can salve their consciences with the knowledge that the 'remedial' child must be better off with the 'expert' who knows what is 'best' for such cases.

In the case of 'remedial education', the idea of 'need' cannot easily be separated from some concept of *ability*, and the most powerful concept of ability has been that of an innate, fixed 'reservoir' of potential learning. It is a further common assumption that this ability is unequally, but symmetrically, distributed throughout the population. The vast majority of teachers – if not all – will recall in their training some discussion of this phenomenon, perhaps in the context of the debate about heredity versus environment in which the former is inevitably linked to the famous 'curve of normal distribution'. It is to be hoped that most student-teachers nowadays will at least be exposed to a critique of the psychological assumptions which such a model makes, yet it is by no means certain its influence on our thinking has much diminished.

Clunies-Ross and Wimhurst (1983) recount how an NFER survey revealed that almost a third of comprehensive schools still place their new entrants in 'ability' bands or streams, while it is still common practice in the surviving grammar schools to stream the intake, even though, according to traditional indicators, even the 'bottom' group would fall within the top quarter of the 'absolute' ability range. The desire to differentiate, even within a narrow section of the 'ability range', would seem too strong to resist.

We suggest that most teachers – and this includes a good many 'remedial' teachers – still work with such a model of 'ability'. Though some may now add cautious caveats of one sort or another – for example, about the degree to which ability is 'fixed' – others still cling uncritically to 'the bell-shaped curve'. The certainty and dogmatism with which this model may be advanced is exemplified in the following extract from an article in the NUT journal *Secondary Education* written by a head-teacher:

> The graph illustrates that 68 per cent of the population is of average intelligence. On a Binet type test their intelligence quotients range from 115 to 85. The graph is symmetrical: thus 16 per cent of the population function significantly above the average level, whilst 16 per cent achieve scores which are more than one standard deviation below the mean. Immediately below the standard deviation, those pupils with intelligence quotients ranging from 85 to 75 are termed backward or retarded. While they are below average they should be regarded as ordinary children, able to be contained within the ordinary school, although particularly

vulnerable to failure. The causal aspects of their backwardness are manifold: heredity; environment; school phobia; truancy; apathy; part-time schooling; over large classes; lack of motivation and, unfortunately, poor teaching. Something in excess of 15 per cent of the population fall into this category. Because they are not innately dull these pupils' needs can and should be met in the main stream of education. It is of passing interest that this approximates the previous submissions of people like Burt, Schonell, Kelmer-Pringle and Segal, who have researched the numbers of people likely to benefit from some form of special educational treatment. I wish to reiterate that this group should be educated in, and totally identified with the ordinary school.'

Curve of Distribution of Intelligence

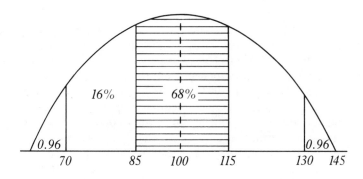

(Sydney Cowans, 1974.)

In fact, this was the opening paragraph of the article, thus establishing the context for the rest of the discussion. Overlooking the patent absurdity of the opening sentence, we need simply note that, despite the assertions that they are 'not innately dull' and should be regarded as 'ordinary children', the entire article is concerned with how to cater for them as an *extra*ordinary category of children.

Assessment and measurement

If it has seemed impossible to think about educational needs without thinking about the concept of ability, it is equally difficult to discuss notions of ability without considering the means by which ability is assessed. It may or may not be that measurement has a particular enchantment in our society because of our commitment to economic competition and exchange (see I Illich,

Deschooling Society, 1973. pp 45–48), but there is no doubt that the psychometric perspective on ability has dominated much of our educational thinking. Indeed, it is difficult to see how we can talk about special needs without presuming some form of measurement. Thus, the Warnock Report (1978), committed to the belief that 'categorisation perpetuates a distinction between two groups of children – the handicapped and the non-handicapped...(a distinction) which we are determined, as far as possible to eliminate' (p43) after all had to assume that it is possible at an early stage, to identify objectively groups of children who are intellectually 'backward' or 'retarded', and commented that it was 'essential...for a child's education that any special needs he has should be discovered and assessed as soon as possible, (p50). This translation of group identification to individual 'special educational needs' does not alter the fact of the distinction itself, and this is a tension which dogs all those who seek improvement in this area.

In the classroom context, teachers' assessments of children's 'ability' may be based on many things. Some will accept without question the assessments of others (previous teachers' and schools' comments, results of standardised 'screening' tests employed as local authority policy, and tests administered by those 'specialists' – often the head of the remedial department – who are responsible for grouping in the receiving school), while others will rely on their own subjective assessments. Westwood (1975) comments on the role of nursery and infant teachers in observing, recording and communicating deviations in behaviour, and how teachers often rely on subjective judgements in the identification of children who might be susceptible to learning difficulties. Westwood found teachers either tacitly or overtly using a 'checklist' of indicators which included such items as:

> less mature
> less ready for academic work
> having poor attention span
> poor at art work
> poor motor control
> poor social and emotional adjustment
> poor speech and language
> more impulsive behaviour

Of course, if needs are to be met they must first be identified, and a profile of a pupil based on such items can be useful. But it is also less 'scientific' than many would like.

The apparently 'scientific' character of more formal testing procedures is, of course, part of their attraction, and there is now an impressive array of tests for measuring (among other things) verbal and non-verbal reasoning, receptive and expressive vocabulary, reading, phonic skills, long- and short-term memory, and creativity. On the face of it, such tests differentiate between 'abilities' in different skills and are often justified in terms of their 'diagnostic' function. However, intelligence tests and tests in the basics of number and literacy predominate, and in these areas years of work have gone into 'standardising' tests across the population – in effect, ensuring that such indicators of 'ability' as 'reading age' are related to the curve of normal distribution. The implication of this is that the identification of 'weaknesses' or 'needs' as a diagnostic exercise tends also to entrench further the whole idea that general 'ability' can be accurately measured and that it is distributed amongst the population in the same way as weight or height.

Ability and causality

The major tension we see in educational thought and practice is between simplistic common-sense notions of children as being more or less 'able' – a notion confirmed, as we have seen, by the cruder psychometrics – and the sophisticated search for *causes* of different types of educational need. The latter trend has led to the growing popularity of the concept of 'specific learning disability', emphasising as it does, the idea that 'needs' or 'problems' have quite a precise and specifiable cause. Thus, it is possible, for example, to identify learning needs which have an 'organic' or 'psychoneurological' root rather than a 'social', 'cultural', or indeed 'hereditary' factor at their base.

This idea is by no means new. In 1967, Johnson and Myklebust referred to such children as

> 'having a psychoneurological learning disability, meaning that behaviour had been disturbed as a result of a dysfunction of the brain and that the problem is one of altered processes, not of a generalised incapacity to learn' (p8)

while Kirk (1975) introduced the compromise term 'learning disability' for the plethora of terminology covering

> 'brain injury, minimal brain damage, cerebral dysfunction...hyperkinetic behaviours, perceptual disorders', etc, which induced 'disorders in development in language, speech, reading and associated communication skills needed for social interaction' (p9).

Similarly, Hallahan and Cruickshank (1973) placed less significance for retardation on genetic factors and instead suggested that 'The problems of the great majority of children described as 'learning disabled'... are fundamentally based in neurological function or dysfunction.' (p12).

Some conditions are clearly more serious than others. Speech impediments of one kind or another, reading difficulties with some kind of neuro-psychological cause – fashionably identified with 'dyslexia' – and retarded language development may be serious in their consequences, yet are far removed from such extreme conditions as autism, deafness, blindness and other severe physical disabilities. These latter will almost certainly continue (at least initially) to require education for considerable periods of the day, week or year in separate rooms, buildings or institutions whereas the former may not. Trends towards integration into 'normal' schools will increase the demand on teachers to cater for the 'abnormal', including those with less extreme physical, visual and auditory handicaps of one kind or another.

No doubt such children will require particularly careful pastoral care, but it is in fact in regard to *socially and culturally engendered difficulties* that the 'pastoral' and the 'remedial' are more likely to come together. Writing in 1971, Gulliford distinguished between 'special education' (for pupils with a 'greater variety of handicaps'), 'remedial education' (for 'slow-learners' of normal 'ability', but having learning difficulties), and 'compensatory education' (for those children whose 'social and cultural backgrounds' retard their capacity for response to education). Gulliford notes that these areas are not mutually exclusive, and indeed the 'conventional wisdom' in some schools is that 'remediality' is directly related to the cultural variance in the school's catchment areas (eg Best, R. *A Study of the Organisation of Remedial Provision in Two Comprehensive Schools*, work in progress).

This perspective is in some measure a result of the sociology of education of the 50s and 60s, preoccupied as it was with the relationship between educational performance and social class. The perception of educational failure as the product of genetic inheritance gave way to a social pathology model in which it was *cultural* inheritance that was seen as most significant. Emphasis on faulty socialisation, Bernstein's (1972) 'restricted' language code, and the social disadvantages of the 'culture of poverty' (Valentine, 1968) directed attention to the 'cultural deficit' with which 'minority' groups of children were considered to suffer.

We suggest that for many teachers the deficit concept is used to explain the need for compensation in the form of *both* remedial education and pastoral care. Again, these ideas are part of an ideology which includes the idea that there is a level of functioning which is regarded, accepted and expected as 'normal' performance, and that special care is required for those whose behaviour must be 'abnormal' by virtue of its significant deviation from that expected.

Such a perspective is not without sense. Given that the generally accepted concept of education is, as we saw above, one in which there is a 'collection code' of 'school knowledge' which all children should learn, and one which is dominated by literacy, numeracy and memory, it is natural to divide children into those who cope with such a curriculum and those who don't. Such a distinction will come naturally enough to many teachers who, after all, are teachers only by virtue of having mastered precisely such a curriculum, and who have so accepted the norms and values of the culture of schooling as to want to spend their adult lives working in such an environment! It is the children they teach who either cannot or will not meet teachers' expectations, either behaviourally and/or academically, who are defined as 'problems' requiring either 'pastoral' or 'remedial' help (cf D Williamson, 1980).

Indeed, Hargreaves (1972, p155) goes so far as to assert that *the* teacher perspective is one from which the teacher perceives children as either 'good' or 'bad' pupils in terms of their conformity to, or deviation from, the teacher's expectations in his/her instructional and disciplinary roles. We suggest that for many teachers, deviation from the former qualifies the child for *remedial* support while deviation from the latter is the primary requirement for referral to the *pastoral* team.

Yet this very distinction seems to be based upon labels which are singularly inappropriate for the description of what we ought to be attempting to do in education. Let us consider these labels a little further.

Pastoral care: are people really sheep?

An early attempt was made by Sean Dooley (1980) to trace the concept of pastoral care to its religious roots and to analyse the etymology of this concept in the structures and beliefs of the church.

Dooley argues that the concept of pastoral care cannot be divorced from its roots in the idea of the pastor as the father or leader of a flock, personified in the story of the good shepherd who sought the sheep that had strayed from the rest. The pastor, he says, is seen as a father figure, the one who must decide, and ultimately in the root word *pascere*, which means *to feed*, the pastor is seen as one upon whom the flock depend for sustenance, whether physical or spiritual. Dooley argues that there is a similarity here between teaching and pastoral care, in that both presume the superiority of the teacher or pastor on the grounds that he or she is both *in* authority and *an* authority.

Whether one talks about a congregation's attitude to its pastor or a class's attitude to its teacher, the person in the position of superiority is there because he or she is recognised as being authoritative in some area of knowledge, expertise or vision. However, there is a crucial difference between teaching and pastoral care, in that the 'good' teacher makes himself dispensable since he looks to the competence of the learner as the ultimate goal of education. Put another way, the 'good' teacher is the one who works himself out of a job and makes himself superfluous by creating in his pupils a degree of autonomy and independence. For the pastor this does not seem to be the case, or so Dooley believes. If we take the Christ figure of the *pastor bonus*, those members of his flock who believe they no longer need him, by definition need him more than ever. Pastoral care at its theological roots, Dooley suggests, implies the need for continual feeding of the flock. If pastoral care is to mean the same in schools as in its etymological origins, then it seems to be a singularly inappropriate term to describe what schools should be doing, precisely because it entails the *dependence* of the flock upon their shepherd rather than the *independence* of the pupil from the teacher.

Not everyone might approve of Dooley's analysis, not least, because it seems to employ a somewhat orthodox and literal interpretation of the role of the pastor in religious communities, an interpretation which many an actual pastor would nowadays be anxious to reject! None the less, Dooley has drawn attention to the tensions between the paternalism of caring and the initiation of individuals into educational pursuits designed to emancipate them from such dependence. This paternalism has been picked up by other writers, amongst them Patrick Hughes (1980), whose short historical analysis of the concept of pastoral care led him to conclude that the tradition from which the concept of caring within education developed was one which smacked of patronage and benevolence.

> 'The moral earnestness of this tradition seems to have combined with the smug condescending attitudes towards the lower orders represented in the activities of such people as Hannah Moore who set out to 'train up the lower classes to habits of industry and virtue'.
>
> Her lifestyle, like that of some others of her contemporaries, has been described as 'compassionate, courageous and unselfseeking'. With hindsight it can also be as clearly identified as self-righteous and patronising. Subordinates in both cases were presumably expected to respond with appropriate appreciation of what was being done for them and with due deference towards their benefactor.' (pp 24–27).

Hughes suggests that the connotations with which words were invested before the combined term 'pastoral care' came into prominent usage seemed to make them refer to this kind of attitude towards others. Pastoral care, then, seems to be a concept out of phase with other developments taking place in education, particularly the ideology of child-centred education embodied in the Plowden Report (1967) and in the works of, for example, John Holt (1965), and indeed with the child-study movement seeking a more reasoned and scientific understanding of how children learn.

What both Dooley (1980) and Hughes (1980) are telling us is that the very concept of pastoral care is itself anachronistic. Is the concept of remedial education any more appropriate?

Remedial education: the nature of the ailment

It seems that remedial education may carry a similar connotation of paternalistic concern. Certainly, at least one writer (Tomlinson, 1982) has argued that

> 'special education is permeated by an ideology of benevolent humanitarianism which provides a moral framework within which professionals and practitioners work'.(p5)

The more powerful analogy here, however, is the medical one. If pastoral care smacks of a benevolence that is pre-welfare state, the vocabulary of remedial education often seems to derive from the National Health Service!

A cursory scanning of the literature of the conventional widsom of remedial education produces an amazing array of medical terms. 'Remedial' itself, of course, ultimately implies something which can be put right, rectified, remedied, as in the case of an illness seen as a physiological function which has gone wrong and needs correction. Other concepts are 'treatment', 'therapy', 'admission', 'case', 'aetiology', 'clinic', 'discharge' and 'diagnosis'. Taken together, such words produce a picture of the child receiving remedial education as one who is suffering from a sickness.

There have been a number of more or less pungent critiques of such a concept, some of which have been referred to in earlier chapters. Amongst them are those of Golby and Gulliver (1979) and Roger Gurney (1976). Golby and Gulliver (1979) identified what they call an ideology of pathology,

> 'which although never stated is nevertheless implicit and is held by both remedial teachers and those who teach 'normal' children. It is that there is a level of functioning which may be regarded as normal; and, distinct from this, there are others which are in different ways 'abnormal'. The condition ascribed to those chil- dren receiving remedial education is regarded essentially as pathological'. (p138)

They go on to argue that this ideology is attributable to the fact that the original thought and work in this area was undertaken by psychologists whose preoccupation with the norm led to the identification of the abnormal as the pathological. As the title of their paper indicates, *Whose remedies, whose ills?*, they consider that the 'ills' to which remedial education seems to point are ultimately those of a system of schooling which cannot really meet the needs of individual children. It is the system which is 'ill' and in need of remedy rather than the individuals within it. In any case, as Gurney argues, to identify whole categories as in some way 'ill', simply because they do not compare favourably in performance with others, is an unacceptable practice. What we need to do is not to compare individuals with others, but to look closely at the situation in respect of each individual and what he or she is capable of. The indiscriminate labelling of individuals as 'remedial' is no more helpful than labelling asthmatics, people with colds, pneumonia, lung cancer, etc, as all having respiratory disorders: to do so tells you nothing about the needs of each individual nor of the different kinds of treatment that such conditions would require.

For Gurney (1976), as for Golby and Gulliver (1979), the whole metaphor is misconceived:

> 'A remedy is usually taken to be some action or substance which restores a previous, and better, state of affairs. But, whatever the difficulties, there is no question of remedial help applying to the diminution of skills which were previously satisfactory and are not now. In other words, a loss of skill is not a criterion for a child to get remedial help. (Gurney, 1976, pp11-12)

While many 'remedial' teachers would argue that they perform their role in an attempt 'to put things right', their argument is based upon the idea of a discrepancy between apparent mental 'ability' and current levels of 'attainment', an idea underwritten by a faith in the concepts of 'normal' and 'abnormal' enshrined in normative testing.

Rhetoric and reality

A particularly strong theme in the critique of the conventional wisdom of 'pastoral care' in education has been to do with the disparity between what is often claimed about 'pastoral care' and what is the reality on the ground. In their early (1977) article, Best et al, conjectured that a careful empirical analysis of 'pastoral care' in comprehensive schools might well disclose a reality less pleasant than the picture conveyed by the 'conventional wisdom' of the then available literature. They suggested that the warm, supportive, child-centred ideology of 'pastoral care' as expounded by such writers as Marland (1974), Blackburn (1975) and Haigh (1975) might be found wanting if one actually looked at what 'pastoral care' meant for the teachers and pupils who were supposedly involved in it, suggesting that historically and sociologically there were grounds for believing that 'pastoral-care' systems performed important latent functions for the schools, functions which did not square too well with a commitment to the welfare of the individual child. Rather, they suggested, pastoral care systems might have evolved to meet the needs and solve the problems of teachers as administrators and disciplinarians. In similar vein, Peter Lang's (1982) work employed the concepts of the 'pastoral fantasy' and 'pastoral incantation'. The fantasy (akin to the 'rhetoric' of Best *et al*) was that schools, through creating structures of heads of house, heads of year and the like, were as a matter of fact committed to the personal, social and emotional welfare of their charges, seeing them not simply as 'empty buckets to be filled with knowledge'. That this was a fantasy would be established, Lang said, by empirical study of, among other things, the perceptions of pupils themselves of those things which were handed to them under the label of 'pastoral care'. Summed up in the words of one malcontent, pastoral care may well have to do with it being 'easier to punish us in small groups'. The idea of 'pastoral incantation' seems to be that if you say something over and over again often enough you will actually bring it about. Again, rhetorical devices may well suggest that children are being cared for when an empirical investigation might show a very different picture.

This kind of argument has perhaps been put most tellingly by Derek Williamson (1980) in his article, *Pastoral Care or Pastoralisation?* In coining the word 'pastoralisation', Williamson has made a happy coining indeed, since it is so clearly reminiscent of 'pasteurisation', the process to which we subject milk in order to render it harmless to human beings! For some children, Williamson suggests, something very much like this is what 'pastoral care' actually boils down to. He argues that there are two categories of children in schools: those who accept or are at least willing to go along with the conventional academic curriculum which the school offers, and those who are not, since they perceive it as inappropriate, irrelevant and meaningless to them. While the former group may well receive guidance in appropriate areas – for example, in respect of the choice of subject options, courses and examinations which will lead on to academic success, further or higher education, etc, – the latter may be referred to the pastoral care specialists on the grounds that they have a 'problem'. Having been disillusioned by what the school offers, the latter group become disruptive and are first perceived as 'problem children'. Their redefinition or redesignation as 'children *with* a problem' justifies their referral to those specialists, who then set about convincing them, one way or another, of the desirability of their accepting what the school offers. When pastoralisation is successful, this group can apparently be safely returned to the main stream of the school's work.

The power of Williamson's argument is that this process of pastoralisation neatly deflects attention from the quality of what the school offers this particular group of children. By defining the children as those with the problems, the fact that the school has failed to offer them meaningful and relevant learning experiences is lost from sight. As a result, pastoralisation serves to conceal the true source of the problem, which is in the curriculum. This kind of thesis is not unique to the critique of 'pastoral care'. Those acquainted with David Hargreaves's (1982) work, *The Challenge for the Comprehensive School*, will recognise a similar thesis being advanced.

The underlying theme in all these critiques is that it is wrong to confuse the stated *aims* of an aspect of schooling with its actual *functions*. It is, after all, one thing to say what you hope something will achieve; it is altogether another thing to establish whether it is achieved and, indeed, whether other functions are not also being performed. The claims of the conventional wisdom of 'pastoral care' are to do with stated aims and objectives which ultimately put the personal, social and emotional welfare of the individual child firmly at the centre of things, whereas these critiques suggest that 'pastoral care' is perhaps ultimately a subtle and insidious form of social control, serving to protect the educational status quo by screening from view the inadequacies of the schooling that we offer.

In regard to remedial education, a similar distinction can be made between statements about what this aspect of education is considered to be aiming to achieve and the actual practices of those involved. The vision behind remedial education gets lost in the practicalities of role expectations. Thus, Edwards (1983, p11) insists that most writers on remedial education describe what remedial education does and not what it is, claiming that there is an inevitable slide from 'remedial education' to 'remedial training or teaching', with an emphasis on basic educational skills which tend to concentrate on reading. McLeod (1983, p24) makes a similar point: that attempts to define learning disability are bedevilled by confusing definition with diagnosis.

Misconceptions

As we saw earlier no discussion of educational need, however conceived, can ignore the pervasiveness of the concept of ability, and this has almost always entailed paying a toll to the whole conception and apparatus of testing and measurement. A substantial literature has now been produced in which it is argued that this toll has been ill spent. Amongst the points which have been strongly made by a variety of writers are the following.

To take the view, as does the majority of the 'remedial' education fraternity, that the problem is one of a child underachieving or not working up to capacity (as evidenced by reading, arithmetic, or whatever, age) is to subscribe to a view of normal attainment in terms of some fixed capacity of ability demonstrable at a particular chronological age (ie IQ). This is unwarranted and ill advised for at least three reasons:

1 If taken on board, Moseley's (1975) view that IQ is a measure of achievement and not a measure of capacity would radically alter the whole purpose of relating school performance to measured intelligence.

2 It is rare to find an analysis of the standards of literacy or numeracy (or anything else for which children supposedly have 'ages') required for participation in the normal curriculum, so predictions about curricular performance based on such tests are bound to be dubious. As for IQ tests, studies by Farr (1969) and Pikulski (1975) have concluded that, whatever it is that is measured by an IQ test, the analysis of the IQ test performance contributes very little to practical remediation plans for academic problems.

3 Such age tests – and, of course, it is the *reading*-age which has dominated the scene – assume that by specific ages all children will have achieved a certain level of competence in a particular skill. Yet there appears to be no absolute reason why all children should develop at the same rate or why those who achieve particular skills sooner or later than others should be considered different from their peers. Unfortunately, the condition, frequently judged by tests, is regarded as one of learning difficulty rather than mere lateness. It is rare to have children under the age of five categorised as learning disabled on account of difficulty in acquiring reading yet, by the time the same child is eight and not reading, he will almost certainly have been so labelled. Because we expect 'normal' reading acquisition to have been achieved by the age of eight, there is a discrepancy between performance and expectation. McLeod's (1983) remark is crucial here: that there is 'no level at which a child *ought* to be achieving' (p24).

In any event, the results of tests undertaken in respect of one kind of ability are often applied to the identification of members of other categories – of which there are many. Bluntly put, tests which have doubtful validity in their proper context have even less credibility when applied outside it. This raises a host of problems for classification of learning needs. As Coles (1978) has shown, for example, there are many inconsistencies within and between tests. He shows that the overwhelming number of children identified as learning disabled in schools are poor readers, and it would appear that for this reason most studies dealing with children who have been identified as learning disabled have used reading levels as the criterion by which to distinguish them. And as Epps *et al* (1984, p99) discovered, serious difficulties arise when attempts are made to differentiate learning disabled pupils from those who are deemed to be slow learners, that is, pupils who fail to acquire the traditional academic skills. Their research has identified grounds for serious concern regarding the differential classification of low-achieving students as either learning disabled or non learning disabled. They claim that there is a lack of 'meaningful psychometric distinctions' between these two groups of students and conclude that the educational utility of the category of 'learning disabilities' is suspect. Similar criticisms can be found in the work of Hallahan and Kauffman (1977) and Kirk and Elkins (1975).

In the light of these criticisms, the reluctance of psychologists to entertain a healthy scepticism about the reliability of their methods is an interesting phenomenon. Thus, Oskamp (1965) demonstrated the disturbing incidence of psychologists who, as they gained more information regarding a particular case, became increasingly confident in their decisions, although their final accuracy was judged to be poor. This is most disconcerting when we consider how much of what passes for special education is based on the findings of psychometric tests, especially when the proposed programme of intervention is dictated by the test.

When IQ scores fail to provide the required result or when intervention programmes have seemingly failed, a common response is to seek further tests designed to probe the neurological world of the child in an attempt to discover irregular patterns to explain the lack of progress. However, Coles (1978) is sceptical of the 'connections' that are supposedly made and suggests that 'neurologists are no closer than learning disabilities experts to establishing a relationship between minimal neurological dysfunction and learning problems' (p323).

Finally, as with the original test procedure, when neurological dysfunction is claimed to exist, there appears to be little evidence of studies which examine the teaching and school environment of the so called learning-disabled child. Instead, as Coles laments, advocates of this ideology would appear to disregard the speculative nature of the tests, using them in a somewhat indiscriminatory way, as though they were a precise diagnostic instrument for assessing cognitive processes.

The sociological critique

The critiques of Best et al (1977), Williamson (1980) and Lang (1982) in respect of pastoral care are, of course, sociological. Informed by the 'New Directions' sociology of the early 1970s, they emphasise the conflict dimension of social life, and tend to reject the simple consensus model of education as performing certain functions for society. Indeed, they are at pains to point out that there is some kind of 'hidden agenda' of subterranean motives, covert or latent functions which give pastoral care its greatest significance in schooling. Similar critiques are to be found in regard to special education in general and remedial education in particular.

The key arguments being advanced are as follows:

1 Testing of ability of any kind, and in particular of whatever it is that IQ tests measure, is not only premised upon, but actively reproduces, socially constructed inequalities. Thus, Davies (1980) sees IQ testing as a political issue and questions the labels 'able', 'less able', 'average' and 'below average' which are placed on children on the basis of a restricted facility to manipulate other people's symbols on a piece of paper, while disregarding the other multitudinous facilities children exhibit. She enquires who benefits from the school's definition of what it is to learn something, and in whose interests IQ tests are legitimised, and comes up with the answer that it suits those children who are competent at IQ tests and adept at the narrow range of skills associated with school success. It is significant that the particular behaviour patterns chosen as being manifestations of intelligence tend to result in a definition of intelligence which benefits the middle class. Davies concludes that the 'intelligence ideology acts as a social control mechanism', legitimising the inequalities of society and defining a person's 'material position within it'. Labels produced through the impact of such an ideology are to be seen as 'selective, funnelling devices rather than liberating ones' (p21).

2 As with pastoral care, there appears to be a correlation between remedial needs and socio-economic status. The correlation between social class and educational success is too well documented to need reiteration. What we have here is a specific instance of that general pattern, pointing yet again to the environment outside school for the source of educational failure. The thesis of 'cultural deprivation' to which this gives support is doubly conservative. On the one hand it legitimises the existing pattern of social stratification; and on the other hand, such deficit ideologies focus attention on the political critique which 'by promoting negative stereotypes of certain social groups...divert attention away from the power system that throws up inequalities in society' (Davies, 1980 p19).

3 Repeated instances of generalised 'failure' – in IQ testing, examination results and so on – for a particular stratum has a significant impact on teachers' perceptions of their clients, bound up with, amongst other things, the practice of concentrating such 'failures' in homogeneous blocks. To a considerable degree, it is argued, children perform up (or down) to the level expected of them, so teachers' grouping and labelling practices, and the expectations they presume and communicate, have the effect of a self-fulfilling prophecy. For

Merton (1949, p421) the self-fulfilling prophecy was a false assessment of the situation which drew a new set of behaviours to validate the original misconception and make it come true.

In their socially legitimated professional roles, teachers are in a strong position to have confidence in their own judgements and fail to see that in the process of making such judgements they significantly affect the outcome. Thus, Leighs (1977) notes that 'teachers inevitably will have expectations concerning their pupils ... such expectations being essential for curriculum preparation' (p318) and Rosenthal and Jacobson (1968) confirm 'how one person's expectations for another person's behaviour can quite unwittingly become a more accurate prediction simply for its having been made.'

Moreover, the organisational arrangements made to cater for such children may themselves have a self-fulfilling effect. Whatever the intention, the outcome of separation and grouping together of children labelled 'retarded' may be double-edged. On one side it possibly protects the child from failure, but on the other it may restrict his or her opportunity to learn. When less achievement is sought from labelled or segregated children it becomes much more difficult for them to return to regular curricular activities.

4 For the school, and schooling generally, the identification of 'special needs' or 'remedial' children neatly deflects attention and criticism from the mainstream of their normal functions. This argument is precisely analogous to Williamson's (1980) critique of the covert function of 'pastoral care' systems as 'pastoralising' those who fall foul of the 'mainstream' culture. Provided help is given to the less fortunate members of society, the education system is seen to be fulfilling its obligations and this legitimises the claim of a system designed to educate every child according to age, aptitude and ability. This is politically very expedient. The system itself remains immune from criticism and perpetuates the divisive inequalities inherent in the present education system. For the corollary seems to be, first, that, if one is not defined as 'special', one's needs are adequately being met by the existing social arrangements. Implying that normality prevails for the majority underlines the success of the system, which, to all intents and purposes, is achieving its explicit goal to educate according to individual needs. Second, by implication, if education is 'special' it must be beneficial or good for the child. And third, as Quicke (1981) emphasises, the distinction makes 'the vital contribution to the survival of the system. It acts as a safety valve, as a way of managing 'deviance' and 'strain' in the system when the contradictions of the system surface and threaten to expose its fundamental injustices'. (p61)

5 As for the individual teacher, it can be argued that the testing, identification and stigmatisation of groups as 'less able', 'remedial' or 'slow learners' perform useful political functions for the ineffective. We suggest that when the child does not learn what the teacher seeks to communicate, this is a problem for the teacher as a professional rather than for the child. For example, where a class of thirty children fails to grasp the objective for the lesson, the teacher

would be at pains to review the techniques and approaches used. However, if twenty-eight children had understood the objective and only two children were left in the dark, we believe it would be important to carry out an equally vigorous inquest of the lesson. Unfortunately, intelligence tests, etc, provide a sanctuary for failing teachers. They are able to accept the test scores at face value and disclaim any responsibility for the lack of certain pupils' success by asserting the psychologist's unquestionable right to label the particular children as 'slow learners', etc, and, therefore, the breakdown of communication is the child's fault. The sop to the teacher's conscience is that once the 'symptom' has been diagnosed, attempts are made with so-called 'treatments' to improve the test score rather than look for alternative causes of the learner's frustration within the lesson.

6 Despite the fact that remedial teachers may be at some pains to point out to their colleagues the skills-related nature of the ability a particular child lacks at any moment, it is arguable that, for most teachers, parents and, indeed, society at large, the concept of 'general, innate cognitive ability' still rules the day. Professionally, it has been equated by many educational psychologists with 'intelligence' as measured on an 'intelligence test'. Both notions are seen in the restricted light of intellectual cognitive activity with little reference to other areas of ability, i.e. physical-manual, creative-aesthetic, etc. The term 'less able' needs the qualification 'less able in certain intellectual cognitive subjects as taught by a certain teacher in a certain way' (Hargreaves, 1980). As it is, a label of 'less able' communicates to the pupil concerned, and to those who teach him or her, the idea that he or she will be 'less able' in *all* things. The child is in no position to question the validity of the claim made by the recognised expert (teacher or psychologist) who has the total backing of the school's organisation.

7 Finally, there is the argument that it is the social relations of the classroom which are the key to understanding 'failure'. We often read in children's reports such comments as 'With a little more confidence Johnny could do well', as though the child's lack of confidence were in no way connected to the relationship of dominance-acquiescence which so often characterises teacher-pupil interaction. If we introduced the concept of 'fear' and re-arranged the sentence to read 'Johnny could do well if he were not so frightened', teachers might be more favourably inclined to assessing the teaching situation! As John Holt (1965) has argued, a child who is constantly frightened of being wrong, of giving the incorrect answer, of failing to produce the desired solution and so of incurring the wrath, ridicule, impatience and antagonistic body language of the teacher (and of looking stupid in front of his peers) is a child who will find an 'open-minded, intelligent and systematic' approach to a problem quite beyond him. He suggests that fear destroys intelligence, that children do not come to school 'stupid': rather, their 'unintelligence' is the result of what schools do to them. Children arrive at school with an enthusiasm, interest and curiosity which so often fails to be capitalised;

instead, there is the tendency to engender fears or manipulate the fears already established within the child in order to achieve social control, order and conformity.

> 'Unintelligence is not what most psychologists seem to suppose, the same thing as intelligence only less of it. It is an entirely different style of behaviour, arising out of an entirely different set of attitudes'. (Holt 1965, p163)

These attitudes are the product of the fear of failure, a fear which teachers all too often use as a form of 'motivation', unwittingly creating yet further irrational and emotional responses to potential learning situations. To reverse this tendency, Holt (1965) argues that teachers' conceptions of learning must be radically changed so that the concept of education as something at which you either 'succeed' or 'fail' disappears, and with it the repressive and debilitating climate of the formal classroom.

Discussion

The picture which emerges from the various critiques of both pastoral care and remedial education discussed in this chapter is by no means a pretty one. Both these expressions of care for the child confronting difficulties of one sort or another have been shown to be based upon analogies that are, to say the least, dubious. Children are not to be seen as 'sheep'; nor is an apparent failure to perform an externally imposed task according to dubious criteria to be seen as an illness. We have argued that such analogies have led to the creation of inappropriate systems of provision, in which the unintended consequences may be as significant and as counter-productive as the aims of the rhetoric are desirable. For both remedial education and pastoral care, the very best of intentions may lead to structures and practices which, at the end of the day, do as much harm as they do good. With regard to pastoral care, a separate system may well create a pastoral-academic split, in which different forms of care are alienated from each other; in 'remedial education' it may lead to the creation of 'sink' groups bedevilled by stigma and ostracism.

Underlying schools' attempts to meet supposed needs are some basic misconceptions. The various critiques of the concept of a measurable intelligence or a general ability, the prevalence of concepts of failure as personal or individual deficits identified through norm-related comparisons, and the downright mis-application and false inference which is often made from the results of such comparisons, are well documented. Much the same can be said of the subtle shift in emphasis from the 'problem child' to the 'child with a problem' which we find in the justification of withdrawal for either academic or pastoral help. To presume that it is the child who has the 'problem' when it is, after all, the professional duty of the teacher to bring about learning, is to misconceive the whole relationship upon which the educational endeavour should be based.

These misconceptions are profoundly significant when we locate them in a broader view of the social relations of schooling. Providing 'special' education for 'special' children is all very well, but if it creates the permanent impression that the mainstream or 'normal' provision that schools make is adequate and successful, then this does real violence to reality. In effect, the identification of some children as needing pastoral or remedial help while others don't, is to shift the attention away from a system which is failing a significant proportion of the population. One does not have to be a Marxist to recognise the correlation that exists between social class and those children who, for one reason or another are identified as in need of something 'extra' (or at any rate 'different'). The process here is conservative in respect both of protecting from criticism the mainstream, conventional curriculum which schools offer and the effectiveness and integrity of the teacher, and of the function which schooling performs in the maintenance and reproduction of inequalities in society.

Within the classroom, to be identified as a failure leads only to stigma, a fear of further failure which is debilitating and self-fulfilling, and a cycle of expectation and fulfilment from which children cannot easily escape. There is nothing unduly cynical about recognising that both remedial departments and teachers with posts of pastoral responsibility spend much of their time dealing with children who cause problems for other teachers involved in the orthodox academic curriculum of the school. Both are, in an important sense, involved in *containment* rather than support.

If schools could admit to themselves the truth about these less than pleasant realities, it would be a step in the right direction. As it is, a traditional and largely academic curriculum, remote from the interests of the children and largely irrelevant to the problems they face in their everyday lives (both now and in the future), continues to be provided to all and sundry, bringing with it success for those whose sub-culture perceives it to be of value, and failure to those whose sub-culture does not. This is not to say that the conventional school curriculum is of no value. Rather, it is to say that it is not at all clear in what respect children can reasonably be supposed to succeed within such a curriculum, and in what ways the present pastoral and remedial arrangements really come to grips with the problems of how to help *all* children to exploit such potential as the curriculum does contain.

Key issues

The critiques discussed above clearly raise serious questions for any school seeking to create appropriate structures and practices for facilitating children's learning, whatever the nature of the difficulties such children and their teachers encounter. We suggest that these key issues are:

1 How should children be grouped in order that their needs – both learning and pastoral – are most effectively met? What kinds of arrangements will

facilitate 'special' help while avoiding, as far as possible, counter-productive labelling, stigmatisation and perpetuation of self-fulfilling prophecies? To what extent is integration possible, and to what extent is separation unavoidable?

2 What administrative arrangements and what structures of roles, duties and responsibilities are appropriate to ensure that children's needs are met as fully and sensitively as possible? Should there be separate departments or separate hierarchies and, if so, how should they relate to other dimensions of the school?

3 To what extent can the needs of children be met by the 'generalist' teacher and to what extent is specialist expertise required? Should every teacher be a pastoral and remedial teacher, or is a division of labour necessary? Is it truly feasible to lay down hard and fast demarcation lines to distinguish between pastoral and academic special needs? Do schools need specialists in guidance and counselling, in special needs education and in specific learning difficulties?

4 What arrangements need to be made for the identification, recording and communication of children's needs within the school, and how can labelling and the self-fulfilling prophecy be avoided within such a system? By what means are needs to be identified? Are *all* measures and *all* tests suspect and, if they are, how much more suspect is the subjective impression of the teacher setting out to 'discover' needs without them?

5 What review, reform or supplementation of the curriculum is required in order to meet more fully the pastoral and learning needs of children? Is the traditional academic curriculum sacrosanct? How could alternative syllabuses/materials be provided without denying equality of opportunity in the context of curricular experience and examination access?

6 By what means can a school raise the awareness of its staff in respect of the complexity of the whole area of pastoral and learning needs? How can the dominant notions of 'success' and 'failure', 'intelligence' and 'ability', 'normal' and 'disturbed' be challenged in teachers' thinking? How can teachers' sensitivity be heightened to the processes of labelling and stigmatisation, (and the functions of fear) in pupil-teacher interaction? How can teachers be brought to the realisation that a problem in education is the *teacher's* problem rather than the pupil's deficiency?

The remainder of this book is concerned with a detailed consideration of these issues. In the course of this consideration we shall draw heavily on the attempts of one school in particular to resolve the issues of the appropriate curricular response, the integration of various kinds of support, and the identification of pupil needs, in order to advocate an alternative approach to conventional models of pastoral care and remedial education. This alternative we shall call: supportive education.

4 The organisation of care

Our concern in this chapter is the institutional or administrative arrangements necessary to facilitate the kind of support entailed in both remedial education and pastoral care. This is not an issue that can be considered in total isolation from some of the considerations of the previous chapter. Clearly, the way in which schools are organised into administrative units as well as into task units (for example teaching groups, tutorial forms, etc), is rich in implications for the separation or integration of children perceived as having needs that are greater than, or different from, those of 'ordinary' children, and, equally clearly, such arrangements have implications for the degree of specialisation of teacher-role that is to obtain.

It is taken for granted in educational management, that comprehensive reorganisation created a need for more complex and sophisticated administrative arrangements, not only because of the broader curriculum that was to be offered, but also as a direct function of the scale of operations in a school of upwards of fifteen hundred pupils. In her influential book, *The Teacher, The School and the Task of Management* (1973), Elizabeth Richardson has described the change in scale as throwing up a pressing problem of a teacher's knowledge of the pupils. Whereas in grammar schools and secondary modern schools, of, say five hundred pupils, the head and her deputy could reasonably expect to know a good many of their pupils, if only by sight, and indirectly know them through the subject teachers who taught them daily, with large comprehensive schools this is clearly impossible. To fill the gap, a pastoral system with heads of division, who could in some respects be seen as mini-head teachers, was a logical response. Whether or not this rational model is a fair description of the complex and often unacknowledged motives which lay behind the sub-division of large schools, is another matter. There are certainly alternative accounts available, which suggest that the need for local authorities to relocate teachers displaced from scale posts in the secondary modern schools and grammar schools from which comprehensives were formed was at least as important a motive as any desire to retain the paternalism of the small-school head. And there can be little doubt that as an administrative device, some form of sub-division of a complex institution is desirable, irrespective of its direct meeting of children's needs.

Pastoral systems

The conventional view is that pastoral care structures which have now become an omnipresent feature of the comprehensive school take one of two forms: vertical or horizontal. Vertical systems appear to have emerged as an echo from a previous era when houses comprised the essential functional units of independent boarding schools. As we noted in Chapter 2, the origin of our system is clearly traceable to the great reforming head teachers of the ninteenth century who accepted that the development of the moral and physical well-being of the child was at least as important as the academic. Indeed, Arnold's order of priority placed intellectual ability third after religious and moral principles and gentlemanly conduct in the pursuit of the Christian ideal.

Vertical systems of houses have often been justified in terms of their creation and maintenance of genuinely caring groups spanning the whole age range of the secondary school. They are not unlike family groupings in that they supposedly make no distinctions by virtue of ability or achievement, so that each member can be of value for himself or herself. They combine people of varying ages in what one hopes is a mutually enriching relationship. Advantages claimed for house systems include the opportunity for the young to learn from the example of the old (a dubious advantage in some cases!), and the stability and continuity of contact between house-staff and children as they progress up the school. Whatever the advantages, house systems have been declining in popularity in recent years, notably because the groupings to which they give rise do not correspond to those groupings in which the mainstream work of the school is supposedly carried on – the teaching groups or age bands that exist for the academic curriculum. Horizontal systems of years, sometimes grouped into divisions or schools within schools, have gradually been replacing vertical systems.

So far as we are aware, no one has recently established empirically the relative incidence of different forms of horizontal system, but it is probably not wide of the mark to suggest that the norm is now the division into upper, middle and lower schools, each with two or three years incorporated within it. Amongst the advantages claimed for this system are that the year tutor or head of year is able to have an overview of his or her whole year both pastorally and academically because of the correspondence of teaching and tutor groups, and that teachers are able to specialise in their tutorial work by concentrating on a narrower age-range with which they feel most comfortable or most proficient.

Those who have written in this field and, indeed, undertaken research into pastoral systems (for example, Moore, 1970; Corbishley and Evans, 1980) have found it quite natural to categorise schools according to this simple vertical/horizontal dichotomy. However, anyone who looks at a number of schools will invariably find that some characteristics of both vertical and horizontal systems are frequently combined in what might be called 'matrix' structures, and that individual schools have developed structures that are often complex and sophisticated responses to the unique and distinctive environment within which they are located, and in response to the specific needs which they confront. It might be going a little far to say that there are as many pastoral care structures as there are schools, but certainly the diversity of structures which even research of a modest scale can reveal is considerable.

In research undertaken some years ago (Ribbins, Best and Jarvis, unpublished), a sample of eight schools in Essex disclosed structures which included gender and architecture as dimensions of the systems as well as fairly straightforward vertical and horizontal systems. In one school, which had been formed by combining two single-sex schools, separate boys' and girls' departments had been created, within which a house master and house mistress were given responsibility for the pastoral care of the children within each year. Only in the sixth form did this pattern cease. This school's structure is shown in Figure 1. In another school, the pastoral system was based on forms located within separate buildings (north, south, east and west buildings) with a hierarchy of role which represented responsibility for either boys or girls within pairs of buildings.

Figure 1

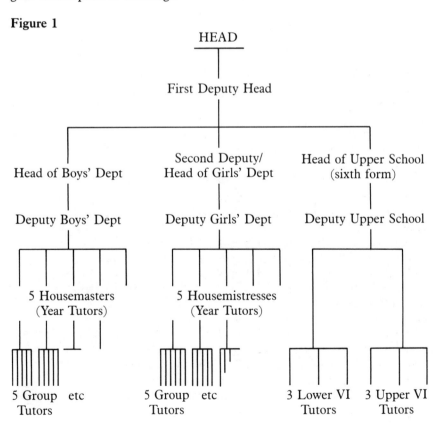

HEAD

First Deputy Head

Head of Boys' Dept — Second Deputy/ Head of Girls' Dept — Head of Upper School (sixth form)

Deputy Boys' Dept — Deputy Girls' Dept — Deputy Upper School

5 Housemasters (Year Tutors) — 5 Housemistresses (Year Tutors)

5 Group etc Tutors — 5 Group etc Tutors — 3 Lower VI Tutors — 3 Upper VI Tutors

Perhaps, because of its complexity, the responses we had when teachers were asked to draw a diagram of the system were remarkably varied, but it was possible to derive from them the structure shown in Figure 2.

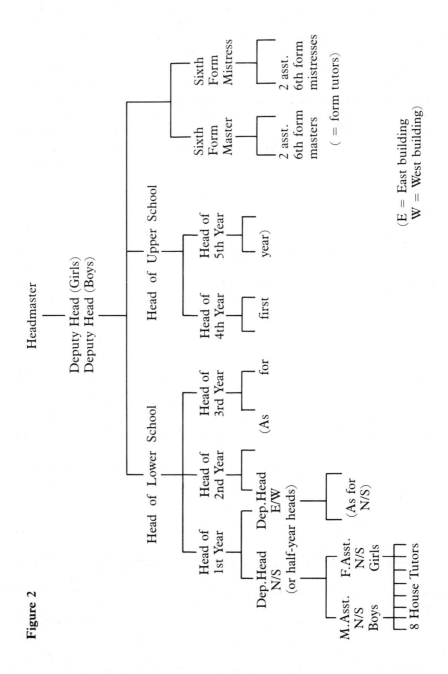

Figure 2

In 'Rivendell', the school studied in depth and reported in *Education and Care* (Best *et al*, 1983, pp 34–35), a matrix of vertical houses and horizontal years with an added dimension of upper and lower schools, which was partly geographical and partly historical in origin, had created a complex system also. As with all the schools studied, Rivendell's pastoral system was paralleled by a traditional curricular or academic structure of subject departments and faculties. The resultant structure is reproduced in Figures 3 and 4.

In view of the complexity of these systems, it is perhaps not surprising that teachers have expressed doubts about the amount of thought that went into the planning of pastoral care systems, and the degree to which they are well or poorly understood by people who have to work within them, or are on the receiving end of their processes. Ribbins *et al* (Unpublished) asked teachers how much attention they thought had been given to a number of issues in the setting up of their school's pastoral systems. Responses were not encouraging. In particular, 33.2% of the 267 teachers who responded thought little or no attention had been given to the relationship between the pastoral care structure and the academic structure of the school; 31.5% thought similarly of the definition of job responsibilities; and as many as 44.4% thought this was true also of the time, energy and material resources demanded by a pastoral care structure. Over 35% considered little or no attention had been given even to the organisation and size of personal tutor groups. Teachers were also asked how well they thought their pastoral care system was understood by a variety of people. The responses gave further cause for concern. 15% of respondents admitted that they understood the system either not very well, poorly, or not at all; 6% thought this to be true of pastoral care staff; and a worrying 38% thought it true of non-pastoral care staff. 43% of teachers believed that pupils' understanding of the system was at best not very good, and 61% thought this was also true of parents. Now it may be that neither the pupils nor the parents need to understand the whole system, so long as they know to whom they should turn for support, advice or guidance, so that the form tutor, and perhaps the appropriate pastoral middle manager, is all the knowledge that is required. However that may be, one must wonder at the effectiveness of a system about which so many of the staff are apparently unclear.

We shall return to the implications of such complex structures a little later. Let us now turn to the organisational arrangements that have been made for the provision of remedial education.

Remedial systems

Here again, a surprising variety of systems have been found to exist. Gerald Haigh (1977) discusses a variety of organisations which he suggests reduce to three main types. The first of these are what he calls *'all-age sinks'* of the kind which characterised small secondary schools in years gone by. They

Figure 3

Curricular Structure

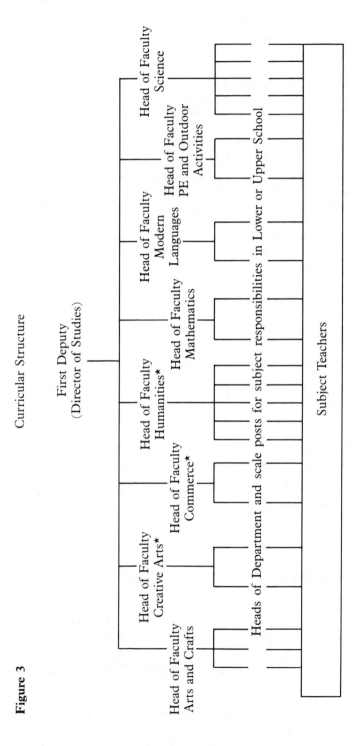

First Deputy
(Director of Studies)

Head of Faculty
Creative Arts*

Head of Faculty
Arts and Crafts

Head of Faculty
Commerce*

Head of Faculty
Humanities*

Head of Faculty
Mathematics

Head of Faculty
Modern
Languages

Head of Faculty
PE and Outdoor
Activities

Head of Faculty
Science

Heads of Department and scale posts for subject responsibilities in Lower or Upper School

Subject Teachers

*On senior-teacher scale

Figure 4

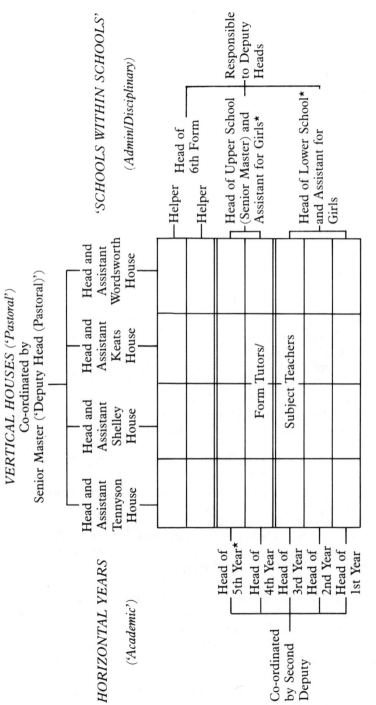

Non-Curricular Structure

VERTICAL HOUSES ('Pastoral')
Co-ordinated by
Senior Master ('Deputy Head (Pastoral)')

'SCHOOLS WITHIN SCHOOLS'

(Admin/Disciplinary)

Head and Assistant Tennyson House · Head and Assistant Shelley House · Head and Assistant Keats House · Head and Assistant Wordsworth House

Form Tutors/

Subject Teachers

Helper — Head of 6th Form — Responsible to Deputy Heads

Helper

Head of Upper School (Senior Master) and Assistant for Girls*

Head of Lower School* and Assistant for Girls

HORIZONTAL YEARS

('Academic')

Head of 5th Year*
Head of 4th Year
Head of 3rd Year
Head of 2nd Year
Head of 1st Year

Co-ordinated by Second Deputy

*On senior-teacher scale

were, we suppose, the heirs of the elementary school tradition in which people remained in a class until they had reached a particular level of attainment, irrespective of their ages. The second is the *special class* in each year 'which might arise simply out of the streaming system, or be created by withdrawal of children throughout the year group' and which is in many people's minds what is usually meant by 'the remedial class'. The third system he mentions is that of the *peripatetic remedial teacher* who works *in situ* with the children in normal classes (p147) or as one of a team of teachers (p64). Haigh concentrates his discussion on the special class in order to pick out some of the advantages and disadvantages of having a permanent grouping resulting from some organisation according to general ability, as compared with a system of withdrawing children throughout the year group according to need. That is to say, he distinguishes between special classes with a permanent membership and classes whose membership changes throughout the day, the week or the year, in the light of their changing needs and the appearance of need in other children.

The special class with a fairly fixed membership may insulate the child from the pressures of a normal academic situation in which he cannot cope, while providing continuity and stability for the pupil, including, in particular, a continuous and enduring relationship with one teacher. But there are clear disadvantages. As we have been at pains to point out throughout this book, there is no one kind of 'remedial child' or 'slow learner'. The special class therefore is not a homogeneous group but one in which there may be diverse particular needs. Because it is linked to some assessment of low general ability, a special class cannot usually cater for the child who is perceived as being 'reasonable', but has a particular problem at a particular time. As we have argued, there are clear dangers for individual children, and indeed for teachers and the school as a whole, in concentrating emotional problems and learning problems in one place. Haigh suggests that this could be unhelpful to children with both kinds of problem. He further suggests that these disadvantages may be overcome by the more careful screening of those who are located in such classes and through limiting the duration of the child's time in the special class.

Advantages claimed for withdrawal are to some extent a mirror image of the criticisms of the alternative. It is suggested that teachers are better able to give the individual or the small group an appropriate programme of learning experiences where this is provided from time to time in the light of particular needs. Withdrawal permits the teacher to start the process more easily from where the child is at. The mechanism of withdrawal permits the teacher to pick up particular problems when and as they arise, regardless of whether these are problems of children with high or low general ability. On the debit side, the impermanence of withdrawal may not give the child with a wide range of needs either enough time or the continuity and stability of provision which he or she requires. Nor are these children completely insulated from an environment which they find upsetting when they are not withdrawn, and where the child's continuous learning in important lessons is disrupted when withdrawal does take place. Finally, there are obvious disadvantages where no permanent base with facilities appropriate to the child's needs is available to him or her.

Haigh goes on to say that

> 'virtually every remedial department runs either or both of the two major methods of organisation which I have mentioned – withdrawal or special class. There is only one other alternative which is in any way different, and that is where the remedial specialist is one of a team of teachers working in the classroom. This method, of putting the teacher *in* rather than taking the children *out*, must clearly overcome some of the difficulties. It is not very common, though, because it presupposes a style of school operation which is still not widespread'. (p64 *Our italics*)

This system of putting the teacher in is one which we shall elaborate a little later. But first a comment or two about the structural units of responsibility which characterise 'remedial' provision.

In the study undertaken by Sampson and Pumfrey for the National Association for Remedial Education in 1970, 90% of the 205 comprehensive schools and 65 secondary modern schools surveyed claimed to have a 'remedial' department, or at least recognisable 'remedial' classes and staff most appropriately described as a 'department'. These departments catered for anything from 4% to 27% of their schools' pupils, with 52% of schools claiming to have full-time remedial arrangements for some children and 45% claiming to have part-time remedial withdrawal for their children (Sampson, 1975, p21; Sampson and Pumfrey, 1970, p103). Class sizes varied from institution to institution, with some classes being taught as a whole and others receiving tuition on an individual basis.

Sampson and Pumfrey comment that 'all these forms of organisation come in a variety of permutations and combinations' (p103). Sampson develops this point:

> 'Most schools arrange the timetable so that the pupils involved are full-time members of remedial department classes, but a few champion part-time withdrawal for group or even individual attention as the best method, while some combine this with class organisation.
>
> 'The situation admits *seven possible styles*: classes only, groups only, individual help only, a combination of classes and groups, a combination of classes and individual help, combination of groups and the individual help, or all three methods. While every permutation occurs *arrangements involving classes in fact dominate the situation*. According to the surveys such classes average twenty pupils but are often larger. Groups average seven pupils. *Remedial courses are normally only available during the first two or three years of a child's secondary school life'*. (p21, *Our italics*)

Westwood (1975) warns us not to take too seriously every claim by a school to have an established remedial department. He quotes an HMI report in the Department of Education and Science Survey No 15 which:

'found that only 51 schools in a sample of 158 had a special department to deal with special educational needs. Even when 'remedial departments' exist they may exist in name only, and close observation within the school fails to reveal any positive approach to tackle the problems of the least able. In other cases (relatively few) one does find a well structured department with wide terms of reference offering a variety of special help'. (p158)

However, a 1974 symposium held by the National Association for Remedial Education produced descriptions from many schools which show a substantial amount of formal institutionalisation of 'remedial' provision and demonstrates something of the diversity of the forms this can take. It is perhaps significant, however, that the contributors were more concerned to describe the curriculum, teaching methods, and teaching organisation than to describe the status and organisational location of the remedial department itself.

One change which clearly has taken place in many schools since Sampson and Pumfrey (1970) undertook their study, is the title under which such departments now operate. As Westwood notes,

'such departments are beginning to shed the title Remedial Department in favour of Department of General Education, or Department of Basic Studies; and why not if it helps to improve the image?' (p158)

Whatever the change in name, this aspect of support for pupils has tended to remain separate from the pastoral care support described earlier in this chapter. Remedial departments by any other name would still tend to be primarily *academic* in focus; that is to say, concern for the child as a pupil or learner first and foremost and only secondarily, if at all, as a person with social, interpersonal or emotional needs. Haigh's (1977) warning that the concentration of children with emotional problems and learning problems in the same place might be counterproductive is in a way ironic, for while 'sin bins' have nothing to commend them, the supposition that some children do poorly because of learning problems and others because of emotional problems, as though these were separable in some way, is clearly simplistic. However that may be, none of the pastoral systems of which we are aware, have ever formally and explicitly included the work of something like a remedial department within either their structure or their remit. Such departments have always been seen as making good the deficiencies of children who cannot cope, for whatever reason, with the work done by traditional academic subject departments.

Let us now consider Haigh's 'only one other alternative: that of putting the teacher in rather than taking the children out', (p64). This is, in fact, the kind of organisation which seems to be entailed by everything that we have said thus far by way of criticism of traditional remedial provision.

An alternative strategy

If we begin from the premise that something called 'learning support' is required by any individual at a point in a task at which they are, for whatever reason, unable to progress further, then it is clear that everybody at some time or another needs learning support. It does not matter whether one is by conventional terms 'bright', 'dull', 'backward', 'gifted', 'retarded' or whatever, it is simply true of human understanding and human mental functioning that the development of our knowledge and understanding is not something which happens at a constant rate and with perfect ease. As we set about grappling with a concept, solving a problem or mastering a skill, we know that sometimes things will go more quickly and more easily for us, while at other times we reach a point beyond which we cannot, for one reason or another, progress. At the risk of drawing a dubious analogy, regarding education as a race, we may think of such moments as hurdles which have to be jumped before further progress can be made. Alternatively, we may think of them as gaps in the path we are following, which must be bridged before we can go on to further learning experiences. Either way, we suggest that at the moment when the child ceases to learn, for whatever reason, this is not only a problem for the child, *but also for the teacher,* for it is precisely the teacher's function to ensure that the conditions in which learning can proceed are maintained.

If we accept (and this is a big assumption to make) that the important learning within school takes place within the conventional curriculum subjects, then it is within the learning of those subjects that these obstacles will be encountered. If we further assume that the diversity of individual capabilities, biographies of experience, emotional or psychological states, personality characteristics, expectations of the teacher and of the school, is virtually infinite, then the possibility of predicting at what point and in what way any individual child or group of children will come upon such a hurdle or gap, or indeed what kind of an obstacle it will be, must be very slim. While our experience of previous children may have taught us that many individuals have experienced difficulty with the idea that the product of two fractions is smaller than either of those two fractions, we must not presume that this child in front of us at this point will also have that difficulty.

If we make these assumptions, then the idea of having a fixed class with a permanent membership who will be taught as a class rather than as individuals, must surely be rejected, whether or not we are talking about a class of supposedly normal children, or a remedial bottom stream. Moreover, if it is the conventional curriculum within which these problems are going to occur, then the idea of trying to identify and overcome them in an environment remote from that in which the normal curriculum is taught would also seem inappropriate.

It seems to us that what is required are class teachers of traditional subjects who are aware of the potential of their pupils to encounter such gaps and hurdles of diverse kinds at any point in any lesson. It also seems to us that if there is to be 'learning support', and if that learning support cannot be provided by every teacher (since some problems require specialist techniques), then the proper format for providing that support is by having such a specialist *in situ* when the problem is encountered. In some schools, this has been institutionalised in the form of what we might call 'supportive education', in which an extra member of staff (a support teacher) is on hand to respond to any request for assistance with a particular need.

Such an arrangement integrates remedial education into the mainstream curriculum of the school in a way which seems likely not only to be more successful in terms of the learning which takes place, but also in terms of avoiding stigmatisation and all the other negative effects of separation. That is not to say, however, that those will be avoided if the way in which such teachers perceive their role and present themselves to their clients, especially in the presence of children who encounter fewer problems than others, is such as to convey to all and sundry that they perceive children seeking their help as somehow deficient. The verbal and non-verbal communication of teachers can obviously undermine the very best of structures. Nor is this to suggest that all remedial and related activities which we have called 'learning support' are to be undertaken in the context of ordinary lessons. The identification of particular hurdles in the normal teaching-learning environment may well necessitate the withdrawal of an individual for some short-term skills development, or indeed some exploration of the precise nature of the need, and this must be acknowledged. What such a system does avoid, however, is the perpetuation of the myths that such 'impediments' are inevitably permanent and that, if you encounter one, you will automatically be susceptible to many others.

Towards integration

It should be clear from the discussion so far, that both remedial education and pastoral care have been the occasions for the creation of a remarkable variety of institutional arrangements, comprising role structures and relations of considerable complexity. It should also be clear that the creation of such structures is by no means without its dangers. These include the sometimes artificial divisions of aspects of educational provision which ought really to be recognised as an indivisible unity, and the creation of identifiable and sometimes labelled groups in a way which is unhelpful and at worst downright damaging.

It is arguable that the concern for integration derives from the fact that a whole has been shattered by the actions of people and the plea for regaining unity is an expression of a fundamental need which, as John Donne's immortal lines remind us, is by no means new:

> 'No man is an Iland, intire of itself; every man is a peece of the continent, a part of the maine; if a clod bee washed away by the Sea, Europe is the lesse, as well as if a Promontorie were...Any mans death deminishes me because I am involved in Mankinde. And therefore never send to know for whom the bell tolls; it tolls for thee.'

By implication, a system which actively promotes segregation has a fundamental flaw, for lacking the totality of the whole it is unable to realise the significance and value of the whole. Therefore, one might argue that any system which adheres strictly to the principle of segregation works to the disadvantage of all participants.

Teachers with vision have long recognised the need for 'wholeness' in any school which is going to achieve its educational and social objectives. In the late 1960s, Albert Rowe (1971) tried to encapsulate this 'wholeness' in the idea of *The School as a Guidance Community*, in which the child as both learner and person felt s/he belonged to a warm and mutually supportive collectivity. This view has been echoed recently in the Rivendell study, in which the founding head teacher's vision was of a genuinely receptive school in which the guiding principle was 'no selection – no rejection'. For him, the key factor was the relationships between members, arguing for a situation of mutual respect between teachers and pupils, teachers and teachers and between pupils and pupils. In short, he argued that, if you got the relationships right, then the rest would follow.

> 'In terms of a school organisation and role definitions, the appropriate structure for the pursuit of such goals was one in which pastoral, academic, disciplinary and geographical concerns were kept together in an organic unity. In effect, the head identified particular areas of the school with particular individuals who were both head of house and head of faculty. These areas were identified with the particular house and the particular subject, and the question of discipline was handled by the person responsible for that area. As the head put it: 'Everything was interlocked and the pastoral side worked in with all the other sides'.' Best *et al*, *Education and Care*, 1983 p114).

The interlocking of these dimensions of schooling has become a major concern for many writers, and a number of proposals for how this might be achieved have been forthcoming. Typically these are in the form of a school-within-a-school. In 1973 we find Elizabeth Halsell arguing that it is impossible to provide guidance and counselling without the kind of experience of the children concerned which comes from teaching them. She made a case for more carefully thought out construction of schools within schools, which would minimise geographical movement for both pupils and teachers, but also facilitate a higher degree of interaction between teachers and pupils (Halsell, 1973). This is an idea developed by John Buckley (1980) in arguing for the creation of what he calls 'learning units' and 'teaching teams' based in a teaching-learning contract. The structure of appropriate relationships, he suggests,

> 'will need to provide for the following:
> i A group of teachers to be responsible for the 'whole' development of a group of learners.
> ii Dialogue between those teachers who teach the same learners.
> iii Decision-making about those learners and their learning to take place as close as possible to those learners in the total school structure.
> iv Dialogue between teachers and learners about the effectiveness of the teaching and learning.' (Buckley, 1980, p187)

These requirements, he proposes, might be met by the creation within a school of stable groups of teachers (the teaching team) providing for the pastoral, disciplinary and curricular needs of a stable group of children (the learning unit), which together would constitute a highly interactive community with a strong and sustaining corporate identity.

The concept of 'community' reminds us again of the important notion of 'wholeness', and particularly that community education has embodied the idea of school and community as ideally inseparable. 'Community' is again invoked by Barbara Cowell and John Wilson (1984) who argue that, in recognising the need for children to receive support, security, and a feeling of identity, pastoral care is really seeking to create a strong and potent community. On a micro level, it is a basic requirement of such tutorial programmes as Leslie Button's *Group Tutoring for the Form Teacher* (1982) that the tutor group be welded into a small caring community (1982, p6).

Of course, if the whole had not been fragmented in the first place, there would be little need to talk about integration. However, integration is an important objective in two senses. First, there is a desire to integrate *children* of very different needs, aptitudes and talents into a single community, which we take to be an essential plank in the comprehensive principle. But this raises a fundamental tension: how does a school integrate a diversity of children while acknowledging and responding to the specific needs of individuals?

Second, there is the desire to integrate the various *dimensions of schooling*, and therefore the *roles* that teachers play, into the kind of organic unity which Halsell (1973), Buckley (1980) and others have advocated. In this respect it seems to us that integration of diverse institutional roles is very much a second best to the ideal in which these various concerns would be integrated in the heart and mind of each teacher. Ideally, every teacher would be a pastoral teacher, and every teacher would be vitally concerned with the educational needs of every individual child. If this were so, there would be no necessity for such categories as 'pastoral need' and 'special educational need'.

However, this ideal is far removed from reality at present for a number of reasons. For one thing, the currently inadequate training of teachers has perpetuated a situation in which many of the professionals see themselves if not exclusively, then certainly primarily, as subject specialists whose task is to transmit a fixed body of knowledge to their pupils. The number of teachers who see themselves as those who bring about learning amongst children rather than those who teach a subject at a pupil is small. Moreover, the inadequacy of existing resources, the size of classes, and the continued demands of an academic curriculum geared to an examination system have made it impossible for any teacher to cater successfully for all individual children's pastoral and academic needs in the context of their mainstream teaching. It seems to us that it is impossible for every teacher to be all things to all pupils in the prevailing climate of ideas and resources, and that the development of posts of pastoral responsibility and responsibilities for special educational needs are most charitably interpreted as the best that can be currently achieved. Putting it bluntly, since every teacher cannot be at all times a pastoral and a special needs person, it is necessary to identify some individuals as specialists in these areas, but with adequate training and resources these specialisms would be integrated in every teacher.

Given the reality that exists, the task of the school may be described as promoting the development of the child through the provision of a set of learning experiences which we know as the curriculum. The child who comes to the school brings with him or her a set of talents and propensities and also a set of needs. For the purposes of analysis these may be thought of as, on the one hand, *learning needs* (special educational needs) and, on the other, *pastoral needs* (personal, social, emotional and physical welfare). It is through pastoral care and special needs provision that schools provide the support necessary to enable the child to benefit from the curriculum. This is summarised in Figure 5.

Ideally, each teacher would be active in each of the boxes A, B and C, but at present such a state of affairs does not exist and it would be folly to press for it as though it were easily accomplished.

The Rickstones model

In a truly comprehensive school it is impossible to divorce the concept of special needs from the principle of integration, but whilst many schools can claim a policy on special educational needs, few can demonstrate that they have achieved the reality of integration. What follows is an account of the approach of one school which has attempted to turn the rhetoric of the above into a practical and working reality. It does not claim to be the definitive approach, or a perfect model without weaknesses or problems; it is simply a description of this school's tentative steps taken along this road. The following saying succinctly illustrates the school's position:

> Any journey must start with a first step. We haven't arrived, but at least we're travelling.

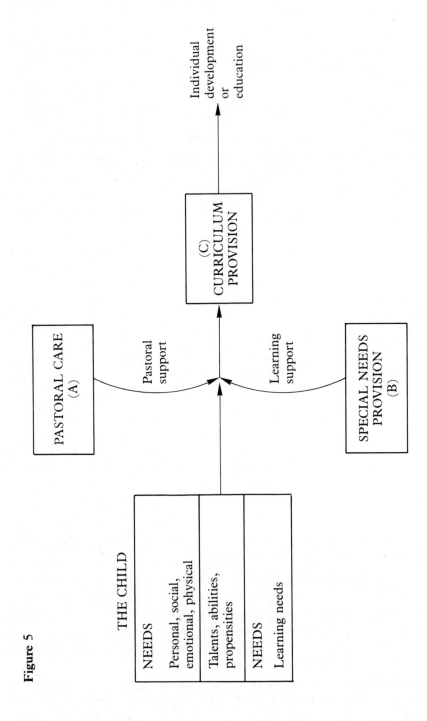

Figure 5

The school in question is in a rural town some forty miles from London. Purpose built some nine years ago as an 11 to 18 comprehensive, the school is entirely on one level (to accommodate the envisaged integration of the disabled) and has a very large open-plan area with sliding wall panels to provide for various combinations of space. The school has experienced falling rolls in recent years, resulting in a five-form entry at present. The total on roll is approximately 700 and there are 39 full-time teachers. Although in theory an 11 to 18 school, the sixth form has now to be shared with the town's other comprehensive, with much of the teaching undertaken in a sixth-form centre two miles away. The catchment area includes two substantial housing estates for London overspill, the town being in large measure a new town round an existing village and, in the view of staff, characterised by many of the associated conditions: high incidence of one-parent families, unemployment, a lack of community identity, isolation from the extended family, and an attitude of indifference (if not antipathy) towards schooling.

The school is organised academically into five faculties: Humanities, Communications, Design, Science and Mathematics and there is a pastoral organisation of three houses (vertical structure), each with a head and a deputy. The principle of mixed-ability grouping has been central to the school's philosophy, although inevitably some more or less informal setting has occurred (mostly in the upper school). There is a flourishing and well designed and integrated humanities course, using key lessons, worksheets (pamphlets) and team teaching in a thematic approach. Although it is school policy that every teacher be responsible for learning and personal needs of the child, one department (Supportive Education) has been set up with a particular concern for meeting special needs and including provision for children who are unable to cope behaviourally with the usual classroom environment.

The school is moving towards a situation in which the needs of all children can be met, whilst maintaining an integrated school. If it is possible to compartmentalise the various parts of the school's provision, we might say that the school's philosophy is as illustrated in Figure 6.

While the work of the school may be seen as essentially to do with the curriculum, separate organisations for pastoral care and for catering for special educational needs have evolved. The aim of the school is to maximise the integration of these dimensions through a whole school policy of supportive education. In pursuit of this aim a structure has been devised which works within a context of mixed-ability teaching, team teaching, open-plan teaching spaces, experiential learning and inquiry-based methods. This structure can be seen to have a number of important elements, including a balanced team of senior management, a named person, a group of support teachers and the integration of the team.

A balanced team

Building on its infra-structure the school has ensured a balance of views by creating a senior management team which at this important level effectively links the academic interests with the pastoral needs of the children. The structure of the senior management team includes the headmistress, the deputy head (curriculum) and the senior mistress (pastoral care), who are collectively (and irreverently) known as the 'Trinity'. In addition eight other seats around the table are occupied by the three heads of house and the five heads of faculty.

The named person

Any system is only as good as its channels of communication, and to this end there are timetabled weekly meetings, involving the senior mistress, heads of house and head of supportive education, to review special needs provision in the school. In line with the Warnock recommendation to designate a senior and influential member of the school to be the 'named person' for special needs, the senior mistress was given this responsibility. In fulfilling her role as head of the pastoral system she is in a position to appreciate the

Figure 6

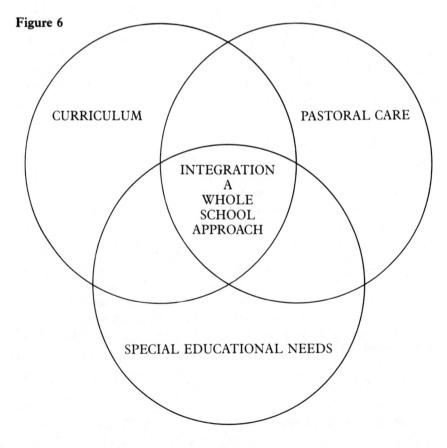

many aspects that might need to be taken into account when attempting to meet individual needs. Her significant position on the senior management team allows her freedom to negotiate and communicate these needs throughout the school and ensures continuity and co-ordination of provision at all levels.

In her role as named person the senior mistress acts like a central clearing house for sorting the information that constantly flows her way. It is through the senior mistress that information is passed to the Trinity, senior management team, heads of house or head of supportive education. It is hoped that this arrangement allows for the free exchange of information on all fronts, from the child's needs, the teachers's needs, through to curricular needs. The triangular arrangement shown in Figure 7 identifies the three points of contact at which staff may obtain information regarding the individual needs of any child. In addition, staff are encouraged to discuss individuals with the appropriate form tutor.

The support teacher

To pre-empt the comments of would-be cynics, let us first dispel the picture of a support teacher as one responsible for the dispensing of trusses, athletic supports or other such surgical appliances. The words 'support teacher' were not chosen lightly, or included as just another euphemistic title, but were deliberately selected to indicate the two distinct roles expected of this person. First, it was felt important to include the word 'teacher' to ensure the maintenance of the professional status of the person performing this role, who, first and foremost, is a teacher of children. Second, it was a deliberate decision

Figure 7

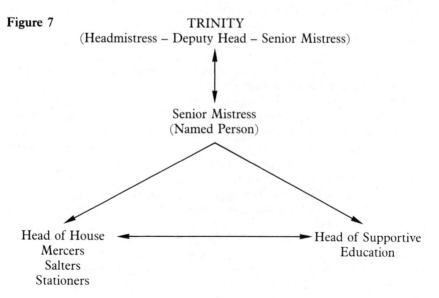

TRINITY
(Headmistress – Deputy Head – Senior Mistress)

Senior Mistress
(Named Person)

Head of House
Mercers
Salters
Stationers

Head of Supportive
Education

to prefix the word 'teacher' with the word 'support' to signify a change of role. The 'support' aspect comes into play to reveal a dual role: to provide resources, guidance and generally support any child, and, of equal importance, to provide similar services for any subject teacher.

This change of role can be a daunting prospect and poses some very real problems that need to be faced (Ferguson and Adams, 1982), but we would argue that in the interests of the child such teething problems must and can be overcome.

The position of the support teacher is illustrated in Figure 8.

Figure 8

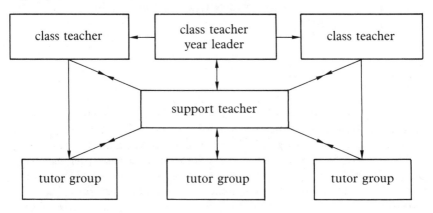

For this school, wherever possible, the classes are blocked in half-year groups and timetabled together for most subjects. Figure 8 shows the organisation of one such half-year for a particular subject, in this case humanities. Each tutor group has a subject (class) teacher, but in addition there is the support teacher to service the three classes. The arrow heads show the possible channels of communication for all participants.

In most instances a team of four teachers will be responsible for a particular subject area in each year, three subject teachers and a support teacher. Commitment and team involvement are the operative words to describe the working of this structure. It requires a commitment to the children and commitment to the structure if such vital processes as the efficient exchange of information along with the planning, resourcing and teaching of the lessons are to be beneficial to all participants. The importance of team involvement must not be underestimated, for it is this that allows a transfer and communication of concerns to the whole team so that, if necessary, it is possible for team-members to substitute for each other's role. In the team's deliberations for the forthcoming theme of work, it is the idea of the child as a *learner* that reigns supreme, and it is with this in mind that the valuable contribution each teacher has to offer to the learning environment is acknowledged.

From the meeting and planning stage we move to the actual lesson where, once the activity has commenced, the support teacher is at liberty to 'float', moving around the class or between classes to ensure that the needs of individual children are being met. At the same time the classroom teacher is fulfilling a similar role, but with greater emphasis on subject matter. It is wrong to think that children need constant and undivided support, for, if the learning environment is matched to the individual's need, then the crucial aim of independent learning should be achieved, so allowing the teachers greater opportunity to sit and discuss the work with individuals or groups, as appropriate.

Integrating the team

If we start from the premise that two heads are better than one, then it is desirable to have a team of teachers contributing ideas towards any particular topic. In this way it is possible to tap the pool of experience and co-ordinate effort rather than allow individual teachers to 'do their own thing' and probably duplicate work covered by others in the department. Moreover, the diversity of experience and specialisms of the team can overcome the inflexibility of an approach which is solely subject-orientated. The year teams have a developmental syllabus involving fortnightly units of work and a shared responsibility for planning and preparing the materials for each two-week period. Regular fortnightly meetings are held for each team and between them they decide content, presentation, types of response, additional resources and so forth, culminating in a draft document (the 'pamphlet') which, if agreed, is handed to the resource centre for production. The resource centre is responsible for all teaching aids (televisions, videos, overhead projectors, tape-recorders, etc), and will convert drafts of work from long-hand into final typed pamphlets and then, using the appropriate means, run off the required number of copies. Departments or individual teachers either block-book or book items on a daily basis. The purpose of such a centre is to prevent uneconomic duplication of resource stocks by separate departments.

As teachers, we are all only too well aware of the number of text books on the market, that for one reason or another fall short of our requirements, and when one adds to this the additional demands made by the particular approach, it is easy to appreciate why this school tends to rely on producing its own pamphlets and worksheets. Whilst some may view this as an unnecessary extra burden of work, others will appreciate the value and freedom this approach has to offer. Once again, team commitment and involvement ensures the production of a pamphlet which should result in a balanced unit of work that presents the material in such a way as to offer activities suitable for the differing skills and talents the children bring to the lesson. More will be said regarding pamphlet-production in discussing the 'curriculum package' in a later chapter.

For the present, it will suffice to say that the pamphlet and curriculum package play a major role in attempting to provide an open and accessible curriculum and, consequently, form the focal point for the efforts of the team.

Having produced the materials, the next stage is to introduce the theme or unit to the children, usually by what has come to be called the 'lead lesson'. For this, all three classes in the half-year group are brought together for one lesson and it is the team's intention to stimulate the children's interest rather than provide a purely fact-giving or recording session. Often the whole team of teachers will be involved in the presentation of the lead lesson which may take a number of forms, from a play, poetry readings, a video recording, a slide show, a film, a demonstration, an illustrated talk through to an open forum perhaps with outside speakers.

The role of each member of the team can be briefly described as follows:

Class teacher If we stay with the case of the integrated humanities course, these are subject specialists from English, history and geography. The class teacher tends to take the lead in supervising the class, but equally the support teacher can assume this responsibility. This can be an area of tension if teachers place different values on certain aspects of children's behaviour, but usually through open discussion of teacher preferences such concerns can be ironed out and have been satisfactorily resolved. The class teacher normally accepts responsibility for commencing each lesson with a short input to motivate the group, and also for the marking of the children's work.

Year leader This is one of the team, usually a Head of Department. It is his or her responsibility to arrange and chair the fortnightly meetings at which the work is planned and prepared. During these sessions the introductory lead lesson is organised and the contribution each team-member will make is agreed. The objectives for a particular topic are outlined along with recommendations for the most appropriate types of exercise the children should be engaged in. However, these meetings are intended to be a 'melting-pot' where problems from previous years, suggestions for different initiatives and ideas from new members are all thrown in for consideration.

Support teacher A major task for the support teachers is not only to suggest appropriate material to be included in the pamphlet, but also to review the presentation of the material from the perspective of concerns for special needs. In certain instances, he or she may be asked to provide a supplementary pamphlet as part of the 'curriculum package'. The meeting provides the opportunity to discuss areas of difficulty that may occur during the forthcoming theme, and explain the additional resources that will be at hand should the need so arise. The support teacher can arrange guidance sheets which provide general routes that children might follow through the work, along with some of the less obvious sources of references. During a lesson the support teacher 'floats' between the classes, responding to specific needs as and when they arise. Furthermore, during the lesson the support teacher arranges short fifteen-minute 'workshop sessions' which are open for all pupils to attend. These usually take the form of a one-to-one situation, but on occasion they can involve a small group of children. The structure and function of workshops will be discussed further in a later chapter. Last, but by no means the least, is the role of updating the records of the child's progress at specific tasks, skills or behaviours. This regular monitoring ensures that a composite picture of the child is maintained and provides a record of successful strategies, resources and approaches that have been tried with a particular child. Record-keeping is always a time-consuming task, but one that is essential if we are to assess needs and respond effectively to the child's ever-changing situation. The support teacher, being relieved of the marking load, is in an ideal position to keep these records up to date. In addition, such time is also used to prepare and continue individual programmes of work in response to specific needs. This division of labour allows each team member to perform his or her duties to the best of their abilities without making overwhelming demands on any one particular individual.

Pastoral system

That this school has attempted to integrate special needs into the curriculum is abundantly clear, but the relationship between these concerns and pastoral care is rather less formal. Some relationships certainly exist in the work of the tutor in the formal period, for here a tutorial programme is taught, devised by the senior mistress (who it has already been noted is the 'named person' for Warnock purposes). In later years this is co-ordinated with a timetabled life skills course and also includes study skills related to examination preparation. Obviously, some of these programmes will relate to specific needs being experienced by some form members from time to time, and the potential to avoid the 'critical incidents' of Hamblin's (1978) scheme is considerable.

Given the many roles teachers play, pastoral concerns ought always to be near the surface. With the exception of the Trinity every member of staff has a pastoral responsibility as either a form tutor or a head of house or deputy, so ought to be conscious of particular needs arising in their own tutor group or house, and it is arguable that through team meetings, team-teaching and the use of the open area, a great deal of informal identification and communication of pastoral issues must occur.

However, the formal structure of heads of house, their deputies, and teams of form tutors have not been constructed consciously to integrate with the class teacher/year leader/support teacher teams outlined above. It is true none the less that the year leader for a subject is frequently also either a head of house or deputy, as, indeed, is the head of the supportive education department. Interviews and observations undertaken by the authors suggest that pastoral concerns have a high visibility in the discussions that go on amongst the teaching teams, and the individuals concerned have expressed understandable difficulty in distinguishing between their activities when wearing one hat rather than another. Like the head of Rivendell, senior management in this school believe they have achieved considerable integration by combining functionally different roles in the same person. The ideal, however, remains a situation in which a total integration along the lines suggested by Buckley (1980) is achieved.

Summary

As Michael Marland (1974) has observed: 'What you want to happen must be institutionalised. It is not enough to rely on goodwill, dedication, hard work, personality and so on'. This is as true of a desire to meet special educational needs as it is of pastoral care. In this chapter we have explored some of the responses schools have made to the requirement that they provide for both academic and extra-curricular needs. We suggest that it is possible, for purposes of analysis and planning, to distinguish between what we have called 'learning support' and 'pastoral support', but that the dangers of creating such divisions as the 'pastoral academic split' are not to be underestimated.

We have shown how pastoral systems in schools are often much more complex than the simple vertical/horizontal distinction suggests, and that structures for remedial provision are also variable in form and complexity. Three of the key issues highlighted in Chapter 3 are clearly visible.

1 To what extent should learning support be integrated in the 'mainstream' activities of the curriculum?
2 What is the proper role of the teacher who specialises in special needs provision within an integrated structure?
3 In what ways is it possible to integrate pastoral and learning support?

In describing the approach to supportive education in one school, we have tried to show the potential of a progressive model of supportive education which takes as its guiding principles the equality of individual worth, the rejection of selection and grouping by some spurious notion of general ability, and the desirability wherever possible of *putting the teacher in rather than taking the children out.* We do not suggest that the Rickstones model is by any means perfect, but rather that it demonstrates the potential of systems which depart from traditional practice. We suggest that the long-term aim for schools should be the total integration of learning support and pastoral support in the context of a whole school policy for curriculum planning.

However, formal bureaucratic organisations are not in themselves a sufficient condition for integrated and sensitive support to be assured, for it is the content and process of provision made within such structures that is crucial.

In the next two chapters, we shall concentrate on the necessary procedures of identifying, recording and communicating childrens' needs, and on the appropriate curricular response to the philosophy of supportive education.

5 Assessment, records and communication

We begin this chapter with anecdotes about two children who are in many respects similar to the Jimmy Stephens with which this book began. Unlike Jimmy, these children really exist and the following events acually happened.

Tracey is in the fourth year of a co-educational comprehensive school with a commitment to 'mixed ability' teaching, integrated studies, and as far as possible an open approach to child-centred learning, project work, etc. Notwithstanding the progressive stance taken on many issues, the school still finds it necessary to hold whole-school examinations for one week during the summer term. For most years these are relatively informal affairs executed in normal class time by subject teachers, but for the fourth year they take the form of a mock public examination. Although the school subscribes to some Mode 3 forms of assessment, thereby avoiding some of the worst features of traditional examinations, the papers set still depend largely on the pupil's ability to read and write. At the end of the first paper (English comprehension) Tracey turns to her form tutor and asks, 'Do you think it is fair that I have to do this when you know I can hardly read the paper?'

Jason is a first-year pupil in the same school. He has already performed well in the practical test in home economics and now sits the theory paper, which is a short multiple-choice objective test to do with the rudiments of cookery. Early items are of the true/false variety, whilst later items offer four or five possible answers, one of which has to be written in the space provided. When marking the papers, Jason's teacher discovers that Jason answers the later questions clearly and in some cases correctly, but that his answers to the true/false items consist of a capital letter followed by meaningless squiggles. This she interprets as an indication that he has not taken the written test seriously, especially as his practical mark was good, and reports the incident to Jason's head of house. When Jason is interviewed he tries to explain what he has done, but in the process is reduced to tears.

In both these cases the situation was resolved through more or less sympathetic handling by the staff involved. Tracey was permitted to sit the next paper (creative writing) using a tape recorder, and although her teacher clearly found it difficult to reconcile this with the conventions of examining and marking, at least everyone recognised that literacy is not all that schools should be assessing, and is certainly not to be equated with the ability to plan and compose a piece of prose. As for Jason, his interview revealed that he could not read the statements, nor did he understand what the true/false alternative was, so had been unable to do anything but go through the motions of writing something in the space provided. With the other items, he had guessed that one of the words given was correct and had copied one of these carefully in the answer space. By chance, this strategy gave the right answer in two cases.

What both these anecdotes highlight are the very serious doubts which we must have about the validity and desirability of conventional use of written assessment. We are not saying that it is wrong to assess children's performance, nor that the results of various forms of assessment are of little use to teachers, nor that the recording and communication of the results is inevitably dangerous or undesirable. However, we do want to argue that Tracey and Jason (and Jimmy Stephens) will be better served if teachers are clear about the reasons why they assess their pupils, about the different functions performed by different types of assessment and about the potential dangers which records of performance entail. We suggest that assessing, recording, and communicating pupil peformance and need are essential if teachers are to be able to maximise their pupils' learning, but that, like any tool, the techniques used may be more or less blunt and may be extremely dangerous in the hands of the wrong person. What is required is an enlightened teaching staff who are well aware of the limitations of assessment and of the unintended consequences of disillusionment, labelling, stigma and the self-fulfilling prophecy. How awareness of these dangers can be raised is the focus of Chapter 7. For the moment we wish to raise a number of fundamental questions which schools need to address in deciding on appropriate methods of assessment, recording and communication of needs.

What are we assessing?

A major problem is that we are often simply unclear what it is we do when we assess children. We suggest that in the following discussions we bear in mind the fact that schools may engage in three related but separate exercises.

The first of these is the attempt to assess the child's ability. This is what is involved in establishing the IQ or intelligence of the child and is seen as an indicator or predictor of the future performance or attainment of that child in those areas of skill and knowledge which make up the curriculum. As we have been at pains to point out in earlier chapters, this is a dubious practice for several reasons, not the least of which is the uncertainty about whether or not 'intelligence' actually exists as some fixed reservoir of potential. More importantly for our purposes, such tests are standardised and norm-referenced and tell us precious little about how a particular child learns, or what kinds of conditions and services a child needs in order to perform better.

The second type of assessment is that which is undertaken in order to identify needs. By this we mean that in recognising that effective learning cannot occur unless the environment and task set are appropriate, we also recognise the need to identify the particular services a child requires in order to create that environment. Talk of ability or potential is empty unless we assess and therefore put ourselves in the position to provide the pre-conditions for its realisation. This is what many people have in mind when they speak of diagnostic assessment, but the use of the medical analogy distorts our perception by implying that the need is of the order of a personal deficiency on the part of the child, rather than the prerequisites of a learning experience.

The third type of assessment is that to which Tracey and Jason were being subjected: the measurement of a child's attainment in the concepts, facts, skills and attitudes which make up the school curriculum. What the school is setting out to do is to determine how much the child has, in fact, learned. In this respect the results of such assessment may be as much an indication of the successful teaching of the school and its staff as it is of the successful learning of the child.

What has happened traditionally is that schools and related agencies have limited their efforts to the first and third types of assessment. Establishing the supposed potential of the child by batteries of intelligence tests, predicting subsequent attainment in examinations, we make the prediction come true by grouping children in the light of that prediction and teaching them accordingly. In fact, it would be surprising indeed if the predictions were refuted in any volume since the requirement of both types of assessment is essentially the same: literacy and a willingness to deal in symbols remote from and irrelevant to everyday life. Where schools have gone wrong is, first, in failing to appreciate that a failure in academic examinations may mean either that we are using forms of assessment which ensure that many children *will* fail, or else that such failures are attributable to the school's inability to identify the environment within which genuine and meaningful learning experiences are available, and second, in not concerning themselves with genuine needs assessment so that the appropriate environment for each child may be identified.

Identification of needs

It is worth reminding ourselves that local authorities are now obliged by law to cater for children with needs deemed to be special. The essential points arising from this legislation are as follows:

a A child has special educational needs if he or she has a learning difficulty which calls for special educational provision to be made.
b The term 'learning difficulty' applies to children whose difficulties arise

from a physical, sensory or emotional problem, as well as to those who are simply experiencing greater difficulty in learning than their peers.

c There are two exceptions to the above: first, difficulties arising where English is not the first language and, second, children who are sometimes termed 'gifted'.

d The school governors are required to ensure that teachers are aware of the need for proper arrangements for identifying children with special needs, and that where a child in the school is known to have special educational needs appropriate provision is made.

e The claim is that at least one in five children in ordinary schools will have special educational needs at some time in their school career, and these should normally be catered for within the school. Only when other special educational provision is deemed necessary should a formal assessment procedure prescribed by the 1981 Act be commenced.

f The concept of *special* educational provision suggests it is something not normally provided but additional to or different from existing provision in the ordinary school.

g Special educational provision should be made within the ordinary school wherever this is appropriate and where it will neither adversely affect the education of other pupils nor entail an inefficient use of resources.

h In cases where a formal assessment of special educational needs is undertaken, advice must be sought from educational, medical and psychological sources together with reports from other agencies that are relevant in the particular case.

i Parents are to receive copies of all such advice and must be consulted throughout the assessment process.

j Requests for a formal assessment can be made by the school through the psychological services, or by a parent making a similar request of the authority.

k Should the authority decide that special educational provision is called for, it must draw up a formal statement of special educational needs. Every authority has its own outline of objectives and criteria that should be reviewed when producing a formal statement, and these should include copies of all reports received as advice and a statement of the provision to be made. Parents have the right of appeal.

l Finally, once a formal statement has been produced, the authority must ensure that the specified provision is made and reviewed at least annually.

(Unpublished Havering policy document, *Providing for Special Educational Needs – A Guide for Schools*)

Whatever the intention, the 1981 Act has done much to extend further the position of normative testing with which educational psychologists are often identified. As we saw in Chapters 3 and 4 there are great problems associated with this kind of assessment, but schools go on labelling children as having learning difficulties simply on the basis of something like a reading age and then, either implicitly or explicitly, predicting low ability and poor performance in all sorts of other areas. Even the sophisticated teacher who recognises that children unable to read are not necessarily unable to learn will often overlook the converse – that children having difficulty with learning are not necessarily unable to read. How often does one hear the call from staff to remove a particular child from their lesson and give him or her more of the basics? The least sophisticated teacher (and there are many in this category) still thinks that all such quotients are indicative of a fixed level of general ability. Even though the construct validity of such tests – that is, the empirical assurance that a test truly measures a given attribute – is acknowledged to be doubtful and, at best, true only because tautological, the links between psychological assessment and teachers' social constructs of ability and achievement are too well established to be easily shaken.

Of course, such interpretations are politically valuable, for locating the cause of low achievement firmly within the head of the child neatly shifts the responsibility from schools and other institutions in the community. On the macro level, it also moves the focus of attention away from the general educational process, away from the need to change institutions, away from the need to rectify social conditions and away from the need to provide more resources (Coles, 1978).

There is a prima-facie case for arguing that this is part of a general pattern in which the key ingredient is that of social class injustice. Why is it, some have asked (Cippolla, 1969; Carnoy, 1974; Bowles and Gintis, 1976; Balow, 1971), that the predominance of children identified by such tests are from the lower social classes? Perhaps what we have here is, after all, a special instance of a general law: that education and educational success is defined and measured by the criteria and standards of a dominant though minority culture. If this is so, then the tendency to attribute low achievement to low ability is even more easily understood, for an irremediable level of ability imposes no demands for increased resources, changes in teaching methods, or any other disturbance of the status quo. Politically this perspective is profoundly conservative.

Over and against the psychometric model we can pose the phenomenological or process model in which the measurement of attainment or ability by supposedly objective methods is replaced by other avenues (McIntyre and Brown, 1978, p42). This alternative is still in its infancy at grass roots level but is more or less implicitly or explicitly adopted by such people as Bloom (1976), Black and Dockrell (1980) and Black (1982). Basically, the psychometric paradigm comes under attack on two grounds: first, that it is of doubtful validity – for all the reasons noted earlier, but particularly because it is norm-referenced, and, second, because it is summative, purporting to assess the outcome of education when it is frankly too late to do anything to correct the experiences to which any individual child is subjected. This is to some extent natural enough, given the preoccupation with reporting and certification of results to the exclusion of developing and adapting the processes by which those results are supposedly produced.

The alternative view therefore advocates criterion-referenced assessment to be linked to the identification of needs undertaken more or less continually throughout the child's school experience. While continuous assessment is now a part of the examination system, it has not been seen as formative in the sense of providing the grounds for 'forming' the next set of learning experiences we provide for the child. What is needed is a truly formative assessment which is an integral part of the on-going evaluation and modification of a dynamic curriculum. Of course, many teachers are following these principles in any classroom situation when they correct errors, discuss why a mistake has occurred, and refine their strategy for the next part of the lesson, but this is a far cry from a common and systematic use of formative assessment of the kind Bloom (1976) recommends or what Black (1982) has in mind when he states that:

> 'Where mastery learning is used the teacher is required to allow the students to master each sequential unit of work. In consequence, each element of learning in the hierarchy takes place when students have mastered the previous element. They therefore support their enhanced cognitive characteristics with more positive attitudes and hence reduce not only the variance in student attainment but also the variance amongst *rates* of attainment.'(p9).

Teaching and learning involve an interactive process which lends itself quite readily to formative assessment procedures. Harry Black acknowledges the relationship between three elements of the learning process: what the student has already attained (cognitive entry characteristics), his attitude to the learning opportunity (affective entry characteristics), and the nature of the teaching available (quality of instruction). Dovetailing these elements is crucial for effective learning (p9).

Who shall identify the need?

These principles were partially reflected in the Warnock report's consideration of special educational needs. Central to the spirit of Warnock is the theme of assessment being the primary means for identifying needs. The suggestion is made that discovery, assessment and recording are crucial issues which follow from the idea that special needs are discernable. If we take the first of these key categories, that of *discovery*, the report leaves no doubt as to where the responsibility for this lies:

> 'We have pointed out that the large majority of children with special educational needs will have to be identified within ordinary schools. It follows that the class teacher must be able to recognise early signs of possible special needs.'
>
> (Warnock, 1978, para 4.18)

This places a significant load on teachers' shoulders, requiring them to become not only familiar with, but also competent in the following (drawn from the unpublished Havering policy document):

1 Being aware of, and appreciating, the wide range and scope of special educational needs.

2 Being aware of the need for early identification. Allowing the situation to continue in the hope that it will rectify itself or to avoid unnecessary anxiety may only compound the need. (In the Rickstones model, the aim is for the teacher to consult with the special needs representative for his or her department, who in turn would inform and, where necessary, involve the support team (see Chapter 4). Together they should be developing strategies for monitoring progress while trying out programmes or ways to overcome the learning difficulty.)

3 Being able, in conjunction with both the special needs representative and the support team, to indicate and devise suitable teaching objectives at the point where a difficulty arises. One Authority, Coventry, has already devised a package called 'Special Needs Action Programme' (SNAP) for primary school use. Several other Authorities are at present preparing similar packages for both primary and secondary schools. In essence the materials break down longer-term objectives into small steps.

4 Being able to involve parents in helping their own children. Interviews with parents (other than the five-minute session on parents' evening) can be an invaluable source of information for understanding a child's needs and for co-ordinating a united approach to a particular need. (We shall return to the school's need to work more closely with parents in Chapter 8.)

Many teachers may claim already to be doing these things to a greater or lesser extent. If this is the case, we must review the success of this teacher-awareness by assessing the positive outcomes that have been achieved by teacher-directed intervention, and then decide whether such approaches can be transferred to other situations.

Unfortunately, a common response to a request to share expertise on the identification of needs is to give the person making the request some kind of test to administer to the child. Identification of need then becomes synonymous with testing and reinforces the simplistic faith in the validity and reliability of tests, which we have already criticised. To reiterate, testing *can* indicate the existence of a particular learning problem which a child has but there are important drawbacks to its use.

a All too often the test does not examine exclusively the skill it purports to examine; rather, reading and language skills are presupposed and it is a lack of facility in *those* skills which causes the 'failure' of many testees;

b Even where a specified skill is tested, standardised tests identify only the *manifestation* of the problem and not the precise nature or cause of the problem itself; and
c If tests tell us relatively little about precise causes, they tell us nothing at all about the kind of action necessary to tackle the problem.

To see identification merely as testing is therefore to take a very short-sighted view of the issues, and to achieve little more than the reinforcement of a teacher's perception of a child's relative position in the rank-order of a class's relative abilities, which he/she already knew and from which the test results could well have been accurately predicted in advance.

What kind of position should the progressive teacher adopt towards testing for the identification of special needs? From our discussion above, there seem to be three possible policies:

1 No testing at all is permissible.
2 No standardised testing is permissible, but genuinely diagnostic testing is acceptable.
3 Standardised tests are permissible, but only as a means of identifying manifestations or symptoms of a problem, the problem then to be explored using either genuinely diagnostic tests or some other method.

Of these, the third is perhaps the most appealing, since it is indicative of a desire to use in appropriate ways all potentially helpful strategies, though some might find the second more attractive. Both of these positions are based on the assumption that genuinely diagnostic testing is feasible. This is doubtful. For one thing, the identification of a symptom depends to some extent on a set of beliefs about what is normal in terms of the processes involved. To take the medical analogy, we know when someone is 'running a temperature' only because we know the normal body temperature for human beings to be 98.6°F. When it comes to processes of the intellect, there is no 'normal temperature' – people simply do not agree about the nature of intellectual functioning, let alone what would count as 'normal ' in this context. The differences between Skinnerian, Piagetian and Freudian models of the psyche, for instance, demonstrate the extent to which the 'same' mental processes are conceived of very differently in different traditions. What is most important for our argument here is the fact that these differences will produce not only competing causal explanations of the symptom, but even different accounts of what a symptom is.

Diagnosis isn't easy

If there is a variation in such conceptions of the processes by which children learn, are we ever able unequivocally to state that a specific test identifies the cause of a learning difficulty? Suppose the following question appeared in a test and the child gave the answer shown:

$$
\begin{array}{r}
546 \\
379 \\
\hline
168 \\
\hline
\end{array}
$$

Can we *diagnose* anything from this? Superficially it has 'diagnosed' a problem with one of the 'four rules of number' – subtraction – but tells us nothing about the precise cause of the problem or about how to 'cure' it. Indeed, it may not even be the operation of subtraction which is at fault. What can we say of such a result? It indicates an answer we did not expect (in other words the wrong answer), but does it tell us anything that may be helpful to the learner? Does it indicate the order in which the question was tackled (i.e. did the child start at the units column and then process the tens and hundreds column)? Does it tell us whether the child tried to calculate the answer on paper or in his head, and, anyway, are the two processes similar? Does it tell us whether the child needs a general explanation of place value or just specific help with subtraction of units? Or could it be simply that the child misunderstood the sign convention and was not even trying to do what we intended? (How often have we heard a child say, 'Do I 'times' or 'add' it, Miss'?) Or could it be that the child is perfectly familiar with subtraction (e.g. concerning her own pocket-money) but is confused with subtraction in this particular abstract form?

This is by no means an exhaustive list, but it illustrates the multitude of factors that come into play in what at face value seems a straightforward question from which a 'diagnosis' might be made. This, coupled with our imperfect understanding of the processes that go on in children's heads, might well lead us to conclude that no genuinely diagnostic tests were possible and that the first of the options might after all be appropriate – no testing at all! We do not propose such a solution. Rather, we would propose that testing should come to mean something very different indeed.

Let us consider the subtraction problem again. Suppose we ask the child to subtract 379 from 546, using either individual Dienes blocks or the main kit of multibase arithmetic blocks. If the child succeeds in this task, are we able to say that the child can subtract? Is it necessary to be able to carry out this task in an abstract manner to prove mastery of the skill of subtraction? Does the child need to be *aware* that what he or she has done is 'subtraction' for us to attribute 'mastery' to the child? Why must all examples of intellectual development be presented in an abstract form?

The answers to these and other questions demand serious thought if we are ever to satisfy the multitude of special educational needs that at the moment we believe we can identify but find so hard to resolve. A starting point might be to provide an assortment of test/assessment procedures to cater for individual children in which the emphasis is not for mass testing but for a collaborative exploration of learning on a one-to-one basis. Only when the teacher sits with the child and observes, listens and records the child's behaviour and thoughts are we to have a chance of breaking the mould that constrains our thinking on special educational needs.

In such a situation it is possible to observe the child's approach and listen whilst he or she explains his or her thinking on a particular question and at the same time respond to their concerns. It is also possible to take some account of the emotional, personal, cultural and environmental factors which come into play in determining the child's performance at any task. Perhaps the following examples may help illustrate the point we are trying to make.

Example 1

Children were carrying out a science experiment to make a simple clock by using a pendulum and recording the time taken for 100 oscillations. The intention was to discover that, by maintaining the same length of pendulum and repeating the experiment several times, the time for the oscillations was very regular. Most children discovered this with little difficulty. Unfortunately, one pair found that their results varied by plus or minus 30 seconds for each 100 oscillations. For them the experiment was totally frustrating. In response to their results, the teacher's tone of voice and choice of words left them in no doubt that she considered their performance 'pathetic'. The teacher concluded that the experiment was beyond them.

However, sitting and actually *watching* the pair conduct the experiment led to the speedy identification of the problem. One child was responsible for recording the time on a stop-clock whilst the other was in charge of counting 100 swings of the pendulum. Working the clock did not pose a problem, but the counting did. It wasn't that the child was unable to count to 100, but that the child counting the oscillations was simply unable to keep up with the number of oscillations and count out loud at the same time. The experiment was not beyond this pair, but the way in which the practicalities were arranged did not match their needs. By observing the children in action it was possible to identify, assess and respond to their special needs. Three possibilities immediately came to mind:

1 Reverse the roles for this particular pair.
2 Tell the child not to count out loud, but to count in his head.
3 Find another method of counting the oscillation – an abacus, a press switch linked to a counting device, or even a light beam which, when broken by the pendulum, counts the oscillations.

In this particular instance, talking with the children and suggesting a reversal of the role each performed, so that the one who had previously worked the stop-watch took responsibility for counting the oscillations and vice versa, made the experiment meaningful and accessible to those involved.

From another angle it identified the fact that one child counted out loud more slowly than the rest of the class; but whether this lack of speed was a 'problem', something that needed to be improved, something to be covertly scolded, or simply an idiosyncrasy that could be overcome in this particular context by providing the child with the appropriate aid is another issue. It is important to remember that there is nothing inherently handicapping about being slow in relation to a particular skill, and that it is only in the artificial world of the school that such things gain any significance and are allowed to become a major handicapping factor. It is not what the child lacks, but more often a question of what the school fails to provide that is the root cause of special needs.

Example 2

Our second example is one which would conventionally be seen as pastoral. In this case, too, we see that one careful and sensitive observation and exploration of the event with the individual concerned is likely to lead to the identification of the true nature of the problem.

Following a PE lesson for a new intake of eleven-year-old children, one boy refused to have a shower. On the surface this was seen by the teacher as outright defiance and the teacher was determined that his authority would not be flouted on the next occasion. However, before the next PE lesson, the child (and his mother) were being seen by the headmistress and the head of house on another matter and in the course of the conversation the problem of the child's reluctance to shower came up. After a little discussion it began to emerge that the real issue was not the taking of a shower, but the taking of a communal shower. Interestingly, the situation would probably not have arisen had it been a girl, for in most instances girls' showering facilities include shower curtains to provide a modicum of privacy. Not so with the boys, where there is the tradition of everyone not only being in the same shower, but actually enjoying the community spirit. For whatever reason, this child was prepared to accept the consequences of his refusal rather than face the embarrassment of a shower with his classmates. A confrontation would have been inevitable without the chance intervention of the head of house, who was able to make a proposal which satisfied both parties without either appearing to lose face.

With some misgivings the PE teacher accepted the alternative of allowing the child to take an early shower at the end of the lesson before the other boys were dismissed from the lesson. In fact, the PE teacher helped to reduce any resentment from his peers by nominating several pupils to perform monitor roles and, for the boy in question, his task was to go in early and 'run' the showers, which carried with it the privilege of taking an early shower. While the cause of the problem – if modesty *is* a problem – has still not been revealed, at least the *nature* of the problem has now been diagnosed.

Records and communication

Key problems confronting any attempt to identify and diagnose needs requiring either academic and pastoral support, or both, are those of labelling and the 'self-fulfilling prophecy'. These were discussed at some length in Chapter 3. Although the Rickstones model of supportive education outlined in the previous chapter provides a structure which might minimise the problem, we still have to face the need to record and communicate the information about such needs to those who not only have a right to know but whose ability to provide support depends upon the quality and quantity of information they receive.

This is not the place to review the various developments which have taken place in this regard over recent years; it has, in any case, been recently undertaken by others (e.g. A Hargreaves, 1985; P Broadfoot, 1985). Those wishing to consider the official line should look to the DES/Welsh Office revised document, *Records of achievement: a statement of policy*, HMSO, 1984. We shall limit ourselves to some observations about the direction in which recent interest in this area has tended to go, and to some suggestions about an appropriate response to the immediate question of monitoring and recording interaction between teacher and learner where support with specific problems is required.

First, much of the effort which has gone into *recording* information seems to have been directed towards three objectives:

a To produce a report of each pupil which will be acceptable to, and meet the needs of, potential employers.
b To produce a profile of each pupil which is more fair insomuch as it describes not only teacher perceptions of traditional school attainments, but also the pupil's perception of his/her performance in such tasks, together with information about extra-school achievements and interests, e.g. hobbies.
c To improve performance by better motivation of the pupils.

The concern has thus not been so much with formative procedures as with summative assessment of each child's attainments and a picture of the product which schools turn out.

Second, such procedures as the records of personal achievement (RPA), the record of personal experience (RPE), the Schools Council's pupils' personal record (PPR) and various grid-type profiles which summarise pupil qualities, skills and achievements appear to be unable to meet all of the avowed aims of such schemes. Thus, as Hargreaves (1985, pp150–151) points out:

> 'Against the success of the schemes in *motivating* many of the less
> able, must be matched their virtual worthlessness to employers
> as aids to *selection*...(whereas) an assessment and recording system
> neatly tailored to the needs of employers may be less than beneficial
> in boosting pupil motivation.'

The efficacy of cumulative records is a similarly thorny issue. Just how much information (and what kind) should be included on pupil record cards and to whom should these records be open? We do not agree with Blackburn (1983), who believes that

> 'The first thing to decide is where to keep the cabinets containing the pupils' files, and who is to be responsible for filing information.' (p123)

Rather, two prior questions need to be asked.
1 Do we need records at all?
2 What purpose will the records serve?

It is only realistic to recognise that schools and their teachers are regularly asked for information about individual children and that many of these requests come from people who have legally and morally legitimate grounds for making such a request: parents, potential employers, social services, police, etc. It is bureaucratically necessary to record such information systematically and comprehensively and to ensure the secure storage and easy retrieval of the material. There is nothing intrinsically good or bad about such records, but it is becoming more widely recognised (as the Data Protection Act shows) that there are dangers of abuse in systems where either inaccurate or irrelevant information is recorded and where access is not carefully controlled.

In regard to supportive education, a number of outside agencies are likely to be involved in meeting the needs of particular children, and the school must be in a position to provide such information as may assist those agencies to resolve either pastoral or academic problems. While we would not presume to anticipate what information is or is not of use to such agencies, it does seem that there is a danger of basing one's approach to a particular problem on a dubious generalisation; for example, the easy attribution of an emotional or behavioural problem to a broken home, or an interpretation of a child's reading difficulties as explicable in terms of the low socio-economic status of his parents. In each case, statistical correlations for whole populations do not necessarily account for the characteristics of any particular instance. All we can say is trite but true: that schools need to think very carefully about the quality and quantity of information which they need to keep in this way. Head teachers who clearly have given thought to this issue and who are exerienced in meeting requests for such information perhaps are better equipped to give advice (see Keith Blackburn, *Head of House, Head of Years*, 1983, Chapter 10).

Much the same problems apply *within* the school: how much and what sort of information should be kept about individual children by specialist supportive staff, pastoral middle managers, form tutors and counsellors, and who should have access to it? If the school really cares, it seems necessary to convey helpful information to those who meet a child in his/her many roles. Some information is uncontentious: for example, where a child has a significant and relatively unembarrassing condition or disability such as deafness, or where a child has a particular learning problem as, for example, difficulty in perceiving diagrammatic representations, a teacher who has not been informed of these matters is disempowered in attempts to help. But do teachers need to know when a parent is in prison? Again, there is probably nothing intrinsically good or bad in such information, but there is potential for both in the way that information is used or construed. In the hands of a sensitive teacher, such information may well permit support to be given and allowances made, while ensuring that embarrassing exchanges are avoided. (How many of us have regretted a flippant remark on learning later that a child has, for example, been recently bereaved?) In the hands of the teacher who believes simplistically in commonplace prejudices, such information is highly dangerous, leading to predictions that are either inaccurate (and therefore unjust) or become accurate because self-fulfilling. Again, we can only appeal to teachers to think very carefully about the quality and quantity of recorded information and the need to protect the integrity of the child.

We can, however, be more confident about the desirability of the individual teacher's keeping up-to-date records of his/her interactions with individual children. For example, where a specialist uses a workshop approach such as that described in Chapter 6, he/she needs to record the strategy employed with each child and the progress made on each occasion. There is a simple practical reason for this and that is that no one's memory is perfect and valuable time and energy would otherwise be wasted in repeating tried but failed methods or setting tasks for which the child has already mastered the required skill. For the form tutor or the head of year the same advice applies. It is simply not possible to keep track of all the pertinent interactions and the insights gained from them without having some system for recording developments.

In the light of our argument about the uniqueness of each individual case of learning or pastoral need, no system of standard categories will suffice. All these can do is to note, at a fairly superficial level, the particular symptom. We suggest that there is no substitute for teachers' own (albeit subjective) observation on each interaction, and we would propose that some kind of diary is the best medium for this.

Those who object that such a record is invalid because subjective have missed the point. In one sense they are wrong because the teacher is recording as accurately as possible his/her perception of the encounter, whether a counselling session or a session with Cuisenaire rods in a workshop and is in this sense as objective as anything could be under such circumstances. In another sense the criticism is invalid since it presumes some notion of measurable certainty (like a reading age) which we have argued is at best unhelpful and at worst spurious. In any case, since the teacher already holds a view of the interaction, recording it in a *private* diary seems harmless and the sheer activity of recording the incident may lead to a greater reflection and improved clarity about precisely what was or was not achieved.

Not that the contents of such observations need always be confidential. It

may well be that such records can help the teacher participate in case conferences, advise colleagues or engage in creative discussions about support
strategies in general and about supporting particular children when their
names arise. Again we must emphasise that the purpose of such records is
to help *understand* the particular need and to aid a sensitive and systematic
approach to meeting it. Their purpose is not to predict future performance
(which our experience tells us does not always follow from past behaviour),
nor to compare one child's performance against some ill-considered norm.

6 A curricular response

One thing which characterised the traditional concepts of remedial education and pastoral care was that they were *reactive* in practice. The school counsellor or head of house was doing his/her job by reacting to a crisis in the personal or emotional adjustment of the child. Whether brought to his/her attention by the child itself or referred by a subject teacher or form tutor, the role of the pastoral teacher was to react to such a problem. In similar fashion, the remedial department was doing its job when it identified (and reacted to) the problems of the 'less able' child or the 'slow learner'. After all, it was not the job of the remedial teacher to stop learning difficulties from happening, but to remedy a problem after it occurred. As noted in earlier chapters, recent developments in both pastoral care and remedial education have involved a shift in emphasis from cure to prevention, and it is very much a part of the philosophy of supportive education here being advanced that neither emotional nor intellectual first aid is sufficient. It is the purpose of this chapter to explore the ways in which teachers concerned for both the academic and pastoral needs of children can adopt a *proactive* stance.

If we take the curriculum to be the total set of learning experiences which a school intentionally provides for its pupils, then a proactive approach to both learning and pastoral support will inevitably involve participation in curriculum planning and implementation. In the light of the critiques developed throughout this book – and especially in Chapter 3 – such participation may be seen as an occasion for considerable soul-searching by the people concerned, for any reform which improves the effectiveness of what schools by and large are currently doing may be seen as tacitly conservative, oiling the wheels for what may be an essentially archaic curriculum imposed on reluctant consumers by a repressive and divisive system. Yet unless one is to resort to the nihilism of the de-schooler – in which case one should not be in the business, let alone writing a book about it – even the most ardent revolutionary must temper his demands for change with an acknowledgement of what is practically possible within existing constraints.

Arguably, the kinds of problems with which we are concerned could only be satisfactorily resolved by total revolution in the curriculum, a revolution in which relevance of learning and excellence for all in the context of equality of worth would be achieved. The reality, however, is a situation in which the demands of many and varied interest groups, the traditional status accorded to some activities, the constraints of an examination system, the proclamations of local authorities, DES, HMI, etc, in their various curriculum documents, and the undeniable apathy and conservatism of many teachers and parents constitute a framework of limitations which only a fool would ignore. What is required is a pragmatic approach which sees curriculum reform within any school as something which is possible on a number of scales.

The scale of curriculum response

Two basic questions confront the curriculum reformer:

1 *What* are we offering?
2 *How* do we offer it?

The first of these questions draws our attention to the way in which schools plan the entire package which they offer children, and it is worth asking how improved support – whether academic or pastoral – should be included in whole-school policies for the curriculum. On this scale, supportive education needs to be included in curriculum planning at the highest level within the school. Neither pastoral care nor remedial education have traditionally featured at this level, pastoral care being seen as something offered over and above the curriculum and remedial education as an exceptional provision for a minority who are at worst somehow or other outside the curriculum, and at best require simply a watered-down version of what everyone else gets. In recent years there has been a growth of activity in the pastoral sphere which has to some extent been incapsulated in Michael Marland's (1980) call for a pastoral curriculum. What is demanded is an across-the-curriculum approach to pastoral care, such that a consideration of tutorial programmes and subjects with a pastoral flavour (for example health education, PSE and careers guidance) are considered alongside such conventional subjects as history, English and drama as possible vehicles for proactive pastoral care. The kind of integration of academic support described in Chapter 4 can be seen as the remedial equivalent: if learning needs are to be met and learning problems overcome and, more importantly, anticipated and avoided, then this too needs to be built in to a total curriculum package which the school offers.

How such whole-school policies should be articulated and implemented is a matter of debate. According to the traditional 'objectives' model (which, incidentally, is the one favoured by Marland in his *Pastoral Curriculum* paper), a school should first specify exactly what, in the way of facts, concepts, skills and attitudes, it wishes children to have, then devise the appropriate learning experiences for their acquisition and subsequently arrange to evaluate the relative success of the venture. For others, a 'process' model is preferred, in which curriculum evaluation and planning go hand in hand, with change and adaptation in the light of experience an on-going feature. For yet others (for example, Stenhouse, 1975) an innovation of the kind being proposed should be seen as an investigation or research project, in which action to improve the curriculum is inseparable from the testing of improvement strategies. We suggest that these objectives, process, and research and development models are not as easily distinguishable as their advocates suggest and that schools contemplating curriculum development on this scale will inevitably find themselves engaged in some combination of the three.

However that may be, schools need to be clear about the scope of their proposed innovations and of the relationship between different forms of support they seek to give. They need to ask themselves the following questions:

a How may learning support and pastoral support be made integral components of the curriculum in such a way as to be proactive rather than reactive?
b To what extent and in what ways can the curriculum be organised to take account of differences in childrens' aptitudes, attitudes and skills mastery?
c Having decided what it is we should offer, what changes do we need to make in the *way* we offer it, so that the valued experiences included in the curriculum are made open to all children?
d What kinds of reactive services will be required to cater for crises either in learning itself (the child who for one reason or another cannot master a particular step in the work) or which impede learning (the child whose personal or emotional problems destroy concentration and motivation)?

In what follows, some ideas about how these questions might be answered will be developed with reference to one school's attempts at curriculum planning. In particular, the possibilities offered by a modular curriculum, the reactive provision of workshops and counselling sessions, the pastoral curriculum, the development of resource packages, the creation of more dynamic situations of total lesson involvement and the adoption of alternative media for the expression and exploration of ideas will all be examined.

Opening the curriculum

Sadly, many children's hopes of making progress through the educational system are dashed when confronted by the conventional textbook, pamphlet or worksheet, which assumes a mastery of reading before access can be gained to the subject at hand. In the *mêlée* of school routine it is all too easy for teachers either to ignore or to forget that an inability to read does not necessarily imply an inability to learn. Even when teachers are aware of this fact, they find it difficult to present their lessons without recourse to written text, and it is not uncommon to discover the level of the text far exceeding the skill of the reader. At secondary level, in particular, it is assumed that children are reading to learn, whilst the converse, that some children are still learning to read, is overlooked. This attitude is not so hard to understand since teachers have themselves successfully progressed through an educational system so steeped in the written word that the physical act of reading is taken for granted. As a result, we have been conditioned to equate *learning* with *reading* and, over many years, we have internalised and come to depend on written material as the only umbilical cord in our teaching. How children fare with reading, therefore, can play an important part in deciding the route they follow through the educational system, for it would seem to us that often it is not their skill at learning that is valued, but rather their skill in reading.

Perhaps it is time to question the supremacy reading has achieved as the almost exclusive medium for promoting learning, for in an era of such tremendous technological advances it seems absurd to continue to rely so much on an approach which promotes failure. Rather than persist with teaching methods and materials which isolate many children from what schools have to offer, we should be seeking means by which the curriculum may be *opened* to all-comers.

Or should we? It is no longer (if it ever was) unduly cynical to suggest that there are political motives in being selective about what is open to whom. A DES official is reputed recently to have said:

> 'There has to be selection because we are beginning to create aspirations which society cannot match... If we have a highly educated and highly idle population we may possibly anticipate more serious social conflict. People must be educated once more to know their place.'
>
> Maureen O'Connor, *The Guardian*, 20.8.85

Such a view clearly subordinates any comprehensive ideal to what are perceived as more pressing needs of social control, a retrograde step into a neo-Victorian era in which the schooling system is required to lock people into their niche in an iniquitous structure of social and occupational classes. In such a climate demands to open the curriculum may seem hopelessly naive and idealistic, but we argue that schools must exploit to the maximum such 'space' as they still have within an increasingly centralised system. A more enlightened approach to the variety of ways in which the curriculum can be presented to children is necessary in order to use this space to the full.

Fortunately, not everyone accepts the reactionary views outlined above. According to the 1985 International Congress on Special Education (Hackett, TES, 9.8.85) schools have indicated a commitment to integration as an important plank of the comprehensive principle, but a major obstacle in its path is a 'shortage of knowledge on ways to deliver the curriculum to children with special needs'. It is not enough to engage in curriculum development or reform in terms of *content*: what is crucial is the building of bridges between that content and the individual child. To teach reading is to build one such bridge, but the error to date has been in thinking that this is the *only* kind of bridge there is.

In what follows we will examine alternative routes for producing an 'open' curriculum in which the important activity of reading is paralleled with other modes of entry and participation in the curriculum. Some of these practices are already in operation in some schools, whilst others are put forward as suggestions for discussion when considering curriculum reform. We shall draw heavily on our experience of one school which, while by no means perfect, has at least gone some way along the road.

First, however, a general point about the relationship between educational resources and the organisation of learning.

Resource-based learning (RBL)

Traditionally, resources for learning were seen as the teacher, the blackboard and the textbook, with the child the passive recipient of a predetermined 'knowledge'.

However, if we accept the idea of learning as an active process in which the learner engages with a variety of stimulating materials, events or situations, then we must accept both a much broader and richer view of resources, and the need to marshal and organise those resources in ways which facilitate such an engagement. This kind of thinking has led to the idea that learning needs to be *resource-based* rather than have resources selected and applied in support of a curriculum which is essentially *teacher-based*.

As in curriculum reform generally, the scale and scope of an RBL approach may vary. At one end of the continuum, children working on individual enquiry from a selection of pamphlets or boxes of books organised around a central theme might be thought of as 'resource-based', while at the other, a grand scheme of project- or enquiry-based work using multi-media materials of a school 'resource centre' may be envisaged. In the latter case, not just printed materials but audio and video cassettes, sound archives, computer simulations, slides, synchronised tape-slide sequences and models of all kinds might be found in an extensive range of materials. Obviously the growth of information technology is having some impact on some schools where there is a growing awareness of the potential of integrating traditional library services with educational technology in schools. As Beswick (1977, p78) notes, this requires no less than a revolution in most people's perception of a library from that of 'storehouse to learning centre', but for most schools significant large-scale developments are yet to take place. Neither are the prospects for the future particularly bright, for in the current economic and political climate the financial demands of a comprehensive programme of resource-based learning is simply beyond most schools. For those seeking to develop such programmes, there are some useful guides available (e.g. Raddon, 1984), though we would suggest that more modest initiatives might be more realistic for many teachers in the present circumstances.

Information handling skills

Whatever the scale of the enterprise and the degree of sophistication of the media to be employed, schools must recognise that children need to be educated in the skills of obtaining, handling and presenting information. At one level this requires a facility in the handling and manipulation of the hardware (and software) of information technology in all its forms – a tape-slide sequence is no good unless you know how to operate the equipment – but there are deeper concerns of equal importance. For example, children need to be taught to discriminate between the essential message of the material and the 'noise' of superfluous detail which simply gets in the way.

Every increase in emphasis on the child as the active agent in a process of enquiry is a louder demand for teaching children precisely such skills. Conventionally, schools have at least paid lip-service to library skills, but a few sessions on the Dewey decimal system and the physical layout of the school-library are no longer (if they ever were) sufficient. Library skills are beginning to give way to 'information-handling skills', and this is to be applauded. For the child experiencing difficulties with learning of one sort or another, there are obviously greater areas of concern. The Dewey classification, after all, is as dependent on logic and numeracy as the book is on one's ability to read, and it may be necessary to cover quite a lot of arithmetic before your library lesson proper can be effective.

Indeed, the child in need of conventional academic support is going to be in even greater need of it in the context of library- or resource-based learning, and the whole question of the appropriateness of the level and presentation of content in the resources becomes especially significant. Moreover, the child with a long history of failure in the academic requirements of the curriculum is likely to be timid and over-awed by the demands of self-directed learning in an alien and threatening environment. While those who run resource centres or libraries may not see them in this way, we are convinced that many children do. The fear of failure, of getting it wrong, of looking stupid and incurring the teacher/librarian's displeasure by being unable to locate or operate a particular book or resource is as serious an impediment to learning as an inability to read the printed word on the blackboard of the chalk-and-talk teacher. Some sensitive and thoughtful pastoral work is going to be a necessary component of any shift away from the conventional classroom context.

Somewhere between the mechanics and specificity of library skills and the broad sweep of information-handling skills, is the concept of study skills. Many schools recognise that the demands of the examination system make essential some kind of instruction in how to revise, and in what kinds of technique are required for adequate performance in the examination room. But this, too, is to simplify (and trivialise) the kinds of skill which children need if they are to handle adequately the information coming at them from a battery of sources. In answer to the question 'What should be taught?' Anne Irving (1982) has summarised these study skills as follows:

a formulating and analysing the range and nature of information
to be gathered
b identifying and appraising the most likely sources
c tracing and finding sources

d examining, selecting and rejecting what is found
e using or interrogating resources
f making notes or otherwise recording any information found
g interpreting, analysing, synthesising and evaluating information
h presenting and communicating information in an organised way
i evaluating personal performance to improve future efficiency

She goes on to say:

'Within each broad category will be found many sub-skills associated with reading, writing, listening, speaking, drawing and generally organising both time, topic and material: writing essays, using libraries, reading textbooks, using computerised information, problem-solving in maths and science, weighing evidence in history, producing graphs and tables in geography, interpreting meaning in literature, and other skills so often assumed or anticipated in the teaching/learning process. The shortest answer of all to the question is to state that study skills are any and all of cognitive and manual activities taking place whenever anyone settles down to acquire knowledge or information.'

(Irving, 1982, p4)

A comprehensive set of skills indeed! For Douglas Hamblin, self-analysis and self-evaluation are as important as (or more important than) the mechanics of revising, summarising and so on. For instance, *Guidance 16–19* (Hamblin, 1983) gives examples of exercises in which pupils can reflect on their attitudes to learning and their relationships to fellow-learners and to teachers, as well as activities to encourage a logical, systematic and rigorous approach to learning materials. He argues that enquiry and problem-solving are appropriate foci for learning procedures for children of all ages – but especially for the older pupil – and goes on to explore the value of using summary and flow diagrams, structured reading, constructive questioning and a facility in the use of evidence in fostering learning amongst the 16–19 age group. However, research shows that the introduction of study skills and related library and information skills concerned with independent learning is not always an unqualified success. An NFER (1983) study, for example, shows that 16+ students largely welcomed study skills:

'...they recognised the need for advice or guidance particularly in getting down to work, concentrating, revising, writing essays or reports, taking notes and making notes, and in developing a good factual memory.'

(R. Tabberer and J. Allman, 1983, p159)

However, the provision of study skills courses did not reduce the anxiety of many of the students researched, and 40 to 50% of some categories of student assessed their value as 'not at all helpful or helpful only in a few respects'.

This is not to say that initiatives in study skills should be abandoned. Rather, schools need to look very carefully at the programmes they do provide to see how they can be more effectively planned and organised to relate to the real anxieties of students.

Tutorial programmes

Clearly, both attitudes and self-awareness and a facility with the practical skills of receiving, sifting, manipulating, ordering and presenting material are important skills to be developed. Equally clearly, they cannot easily be divorced from each other. Difficulties with skills-related learning tasks can seriously affect a child's confidence and will to persevere, and the end of the well-adjusted and secure person to which the pastoral endeavour is directed is threatened by insensitive academic demands for which the prerequisite skills have not been provided. Indeed, Douglas Hamblin's earlier books (notably *The Teacher and Pastoral Care*, 1978) advocate a pastoral care provision which is organised in the light of critical incidents in the child's (academic) school career such as option choices and examination preparation. To neglect the impact of the pressures of the curriculum on the child as a person is as short-sighted as the neglect of the impact of personal, social or emotional problems on the child as a *learner*. The result in each case may be the precipitation of a crisis which could have been avoided.

Not surprisingly, therefore, study-skills are to be found cheek-by-jowl with exercises in personal and social development in such tutorial programmes as the Lancashire *Active Tutorial Work* series (Baldwin and Wells, 1979–1981) and Leslie Button's *Group Tutoring for the Form Teacher* (1981–2), as well as in Hamblin's own offerings on pastoral care. However, as we hinted in an earlier chapter, there are dangers in an unreflective acceptance of conventional study skills into the pastoral curriculum. Unless this is carefully thought out and implemented in relation to other (pastoral) concerns, the net result may again be the subversion of a well-intentioned programme for personal and social education by what is, in the last analysis, yet another instance of the dominance of the demands of the academic curriculum.

Conceived more broadly, the pastoral curriculum is an altogether more significant development than the advent of structured tutorial programmes, encompassing also those parts of the curriculum more often seen as health, social, careers or moral education. More recently, the development of programmes in life and social skills and personal and social education may be seen as an important move towards a holistically conceived pastoral or 'welfare' curriculum. In the planning of initiatives in these areas, schools need to be clear not only about the *aims* of such programmes and the details of by whom and by what methods they will be taught, but also of the intended scope of the innovation. Are they to go for an 'across the curriculum' approach, in which subjects with a pastoral flavour are rationalised and synthesised, or is a more limited tutorial programme to be the goal?

We shall not elaborate these issues here, but rather direct our attention to the means by which more *academic* support has been provided in one school.

'Opening' the curriculum in Rickstones School

A number of strategies or procedures have been adopted specifically to provide support in the context of the overall school philosophy described in Chapter 4. The first of these procedures involves the *resource package*. In this we describe how children can be integrated into the mainstream and join in the activities enjoyed by their classmates without segregation. Second, we will discuss a practice called the *workshop* which has been developed and has enjoyed success in the school in its attempts to provide a service for all children without resorting to invidious labelling. Finally, consideration will be given to the idea of a *modular curriculum* (championed by such progressive authorities as Hargreaves, 1984) and recently considered in a prestigious seminar organised by the Schools Curriculum Development Committee (1986), and which, once again, has been piloted on a limited scale in the school.

Let us consider each of these in turn, noting as we do so the steps which need to be taken to ensure the accessibility and utility of the medium to the learner.

The pamphlet and resource package

As the title implies, we are talking about an actual package of materials or resources which are designed to increase the accessibility of the curriculum. In the integrated humanities course these packages are a supplement to a sophisticated worksheet or pamphlet which is a major teaching medium. For each topic on the syllabus there are several copies of a package freely available to all pupils. During the course of a topic most children at some time will glance at the contents of the appropriate package and take out an item.

At first glance there is nothing particularly striking about such an arrangement; after all, worksheets, Jackdaws and other project folders have been around for donkey's years. However, a survey of the frequency of use of such resources across the nation's schools might show that they are by no means as popular as one might suppose. Nor are their contents necessarily either particularly stimulating or carefully chosen. The resources of each package must be carefully selected to include items of interest to satisfy many of the diverse needs which present themselves in any lesson. Moreover, the package must be a *dynamic* resource rather than a static one and is therefore continually updated to accommodate new needs as they are recognised.

It is also necessary to provide such a range of material as to attract most, if not all, children at some time in the life of the topic. This is not only because variety is as desirable for the 'high flier' as for the poor reader, but also because it reduces the danger of stigmatisation of the child who might otherwise be identified as a constant or regular user of 'easy' materials. The aim is for the package to be seen as a general resource, an annex or supplement to the main pamphlet, which has the potential to be a central retrieval file with something in it for everyone.

Given its dynamic nature, it is difficult to specify precisely what any resource package might at any one time contain, but a typical package would contain:

- a reference sheet directing the child to various sources for material, giving book names, pages, etc
- the main pamphlet
- one or more supplementary pamphlets with controlled vocabulary and many illustrations (possibly printed in 'jumbo' type-face)
- an audio cassette related to one or both of the pamphlets
- banda'd sheets for cutting out/colouring/reproducing illustrations
- a reference to a video cassette to be collected from the school or county resource centre
- reference to raw materials for model-making

Whatever the precise content of a particular package, serious attention will have been given to three considerations in its selection and organisation. These are:

1 the principle of good presentation
2 the potential of the fifth R – the 'recorder'
3 the implications for lesson involvement

1 The principle of good presentation What we are suggesting is not some revolutionary or earth-shattering revelation, but simply the introduction into curriculum reform of a practice performed millions of times each day in newsagents' shops throughout the length and breadth of this country. From dawn to dusk citizens enter and select the paper they prefer from a range displayed on the newsagent's counter. In the popularity stakes the *Daily Mirror* far exceeds the *Guardian* in its sales, just as the *Sun* is a straight winner when competing with *The Times*, and whilst it could be argued that each pair of papers may have similar political leanings, the readers would appear to base their selection on more obvious features. Whilst all these papers cover the same major stories, their styles vary considerably and it would seem that the reader's choice of paper rests on such qualities as its layout, depth/sensational aspect of reporting, and illustrative matter.

We suggest that this element of choice is one thing which is missing when material is presented to children. Surely it is understandable if some children 'switch off' when no alternatives are offered or if, on the odd occasion where a choice is available, it is (to pursue the analogy) to be made from among *The Times*, *The Financial Times* or *The Sunday Times*. Each of these newspapers may be fine in its own right but, as sales figures show, if the intention is to reach the whole of the audience, a balance is required which includes approaches similar to those found in the *Sun*, *Daily Mirror* and *Today*, along with the late lamented pictorial papers and, we may add, the comics. Only when this stage is reached can it be said that a genuine choice is on offer. For each topic there will be at least two pamphlets which, although covering essentially the same issues and directed towards a common objective, vary considerably in style of presentation. In seeking successful presentation, attention needs to be given to four things: predictability, typography, structure and layout.

Predictability When one is confronted with a page of text, the task of decoding and understanding it depends, to a large extent, on the reader's ease in predicting what is coming next, with regard both to the sequence of words on the page and to the intended meaning of the text. To assist the child in his/her efforts to read the material it can be helpful to break the text into small sections, no more than a paragraph in length, and accompany each piece of text with an appropriate picture, sketch or other form of illustration. The reader is helped in his/her understanding of the material by taking advantage of the cues given by the pictures rather than by relying solely on the text. Examples of this approach are to be found in car manuals, some recipe books and the good old comic, but its influence can also be witnessed amongst the more popular tabloids, where a great deal of emphasis is placed on graphic representations, often using a series of pictures to unfold the story.

For the teacher, finding a source of suitable illustrations to accompany the text can become quite a headache, but it is worth bearing in mind that not all pictures are subject to copyright restrictions and some surprisingly useful examples can often be found on one's own doorstep. The long-suffering art department – so often feeling appreciated only when a foyer display for open day or a backdrop for the school play is needed – can provide expert and invaluable support, and every year has its share of talented young artists who would be only too pleased to have their sketches included in a pamphlet. Another frequently underestimated resource is the parents: how many frustrated illustrators are there, waiting for their talents to be tapped? By providing the appropriate illustrations the dependence on the written word can be significantly reduced and, whilst one pamphlet may still take on the standard or traditional textbook presentation (*The Times* approach) the other makes the greatest possible use of pictures accompanied by the bare minimum of text or even no text at all. What text is included should be restricted to the high frequency words wherever possible (*An English Word Count*, Wright, 1965; *Words Children Use*, Edwards and Gibbon, 1973).

Typography In an attempt to convey as much 'knowledge' as possible to the learner and bearing in mind the pressures of capitation restraints, there is an understandable tendency to swamp a pamphlet or worksheet with as much information as possible on each page. Whilst some children are able and willing to sit patiently and sift through to glean the information they want, experience should tell us that others can find this a nightmare. Our knowledge of the eye's scanning movements shows that the sheer physical task of transforming a page of culturally defined squiggles into meaningful messages is for some people quite formidable. The difficulty of this procedure can be unwittingly increased in the teacher's eagerness to cram a page with every conceivable snippet or relevant fact. We would argue that a major factor in the accessibility of school-produced worksheets is the teacher's discretion in the judicious selection and sparing use of written material. But the weight of script is only part of it.

One only has to witness the numerous different strategies children enlist to help them scan a line of print to realise that the size of type-face, spacing between words and spacing between the lines of print can affect the readability of the text. It is in this respect that such devices as 'jumbo' type-script come into their own, providing the necessary resource to meet the above require-ments. In the age of the computer and dot-matrix printers it is a straightfor-ward matter to produce lettering to any specification merely by feeding in the appropriate codes. This facility allows a considerable range of bold, spaced and shaped lettering which introduces the variety so necessary to maintain and focus the reader's attention. Whilst some children might cringe at the prospect of using a pamphlet with 'jumbo' print, the dot-matrix printer overcomes this prejudice or embarrassment, and even the 'jumbo' print can be made more acceptable to older children if trouble is taken to copy the original using a reducing photocopier which maintains the perspective and proportion but achieves a more traditional form of print. Typewriters using 'golf-ball' and 'daisy-wheel' printers can add a further dimension to the printed page by providing a selection of type faces at the mere touch of a button. Used consistently, different type-faces can be employed to pin-point important words, highlight facts and formuli, and draw attention to specific sentences and paragraphs which underline or summarise relevant stages and procedures. Of course, the quality of the final product will depend also on the technical quality of the printing process. Whether or not schools opt for an extensive resource centre, the hands and eyes of a skilled technician are important if the use of the teacher's time and expertise is to be maximised where it is most appropriate: in planning and teaching rather than in the mechanics of production. While many teachers may feel these services to be beyond their own school, many (if not all) local authorities have resource centres of some kind. Teachers need to avail themselves of the opportunities on offer, though for many this will require forward-planning beyond that which is necessary when school-based resources exist. The advantages of a properly staffed resource service can be further appreciated when we consider layout.

Structure and layout Unlike the daily newspapers, schools have a captive audience for their materials, so it is perhaps natural that we are slow to evaluate the worksheets, pamphlets and so on in terms of customer appeal. Despite the consumer's rejection of products which are inappropriate or patently ugly, the teacher's failure to communicate to the child is often simply attributed to factors beyond his/her control. If the national dailies did this, they would be out of business in a week.

What the dailies do is to adapt in the light of the market's response so that what evolves is a 'house style' to which journalists are then expected to conform. Some common features may be noted: a headline captures the attention, a picture and caption sets the scene, an opening paragraph in bold print provides a summary of the plot, with subsequent paragraphs in reducing print size carrying the 'meat' of the story. This formula meets the varied tastes of most readers, providing pictorial immediacy – 'you are there' – for some, a thumb-nail sketch for others, and, for those who prefer it, an opportunity to read on and discover the details of what is invariably a situation much more complicated than it first appears.

Breaking down a piece of work into smaller units can provide the teacher with the opportunity to develop this kind of approach, allowing short pieces of text to be synchronised with appropriate pictures and the 'objective' or crucial issue highlighted in a bold headline or caption. This style of presentation can be used in the alternative pamphlets contained in the resource package, bringing the *point* of the content within the grasp of every child. It should be an easier task for the teacher then to capitalise on the child's natural curiosity and to lead him/her on from the opening paragraph.

Deciding exactly how the carefully structured combination of graphical, textual and pictorial components are spaced and ordered on the page is an important but difficult task. Again, practice makes perfect and the services of an experienced resource technician are priceless. Obviously, the precise content in each case makes generalisation difficult, but a number of rules can be suggested.

- Go for variety: as the dailies know, conformity to house style quickly becomes stagnant if the same layout is used page after page.

- Don't over-fill the page, especially in pamphlets or worksheets for children with reading limitations; nothing is more off-putting than a congested page when you are having difficulties reading the headline.

- Don't be too easily inhibited by conventions as, for example, in the case of paper-size. The switch to tabloid by some dailies may have a lesson for us too. Is A4 the *only* size available and is it, anyway, the most appropriate? For some purposes A5 booklets (from folded A4) may be more useful, leaving the child with more of the surrounding work-surface available for the organisation of tools and materials. The psychological effect may also be valuable for some children: smaller pages may suggest smaller units of work more easily accomplished and, for those who find reading a daunting task, this may be the added incentive they need to tackle the task. For other purposes (and for other children!) a larger format may be desirable, with clear spaces inviting bold and adventurous composition and art-work.

- Be prepared to experiment, but monitor carefully reactions to innovation. After all, how often do we give serious weight to a child's response to a new medium or novel format?

2 The potential of the Fifth R Like it or not, the newspaper world had to come to terms with the evolution and competition of other media: wireless (radio), newsreel, television. The educational world has yet to come to terms with the technological advances which have happened since the traditional nineteenth century curriculum of the Four Rs – reading, writing, arithmetic and religion – became so firmly established. Educational radio, television, films and video have all found a place in schools, but one which, we would argue, has all too often been of limited use to the 'typical' teacher, plodding through a traditional and rigidly ordered syllabus. In the context of providing a greater variety of means by which children can be given access to the curriculum, each of these media is rich in potential. However, for the individualised approach we are concerned with here, it is the advent of the portable tape cassette recorder – the fifth R – which has the greatest untapped promise.

It is this we shall now explore by looking, first, at the passive role of the pupil in a situation where the tape replaces the text, and second, at the potential for the child's active and creative involvement in his/her own learning.

From text to tape: the passive role No resource package is complete without a pre-recorded cassette to accompany each pamphlet. This recording converts the text of the pamphlet, word for word, onto a cassette but may also augment the text in various ways. It sounds simple, but the production and use of both cassette and pamphlet need careful thought if independent learning is to be encouraged.

First, while it is true that for many children nowadays, with their home experience and their personal Walkman, the skills involved in playing cassettes are already at their fingertips, this should never be taken for granted. We must ensure that the child is confident with the machine, is aware that its functioning depends upon the user's command, and that he/she has the authority to stop, rewind or fast-forward the tape according to his/her needs.

Second, we need to preface our audio material with succinct and precise instructions, e.g. 'Press the rewind button now'; 'If you are in any doubt, stop the tape and ask for help from the teacher'; 'You can stop and replay a section as many times as you like'; 'I am going to read page 1'.

Third, the synchronisation of the pamphlet and the cassette requires 'markers' throughout both so that the child knows precisely where the cassette has got to in relation to the text. A variety of visual markers will be necessary: coloured stars, geometric shapes, underlining, the numbering of paragraphs/ lines, etc, make this possible, e.g. 'Now look for the red star on page 2. I am going to read this section, pointing out some of the apparatus in the diagram beside it'. Comparable instructions from text to tape will be appropriate from time to time, for example, 'If you want to remind yourself of the difference between kinetic, potential, chemical and electrical energy, use the fast-forward button to advance the tape to counter number 325.'

Fourth, although text needs to be faithfully reproduced on the tape – since following the word with both eye and ear simultaneously is an effective means of improving reading – opportunities to supplement or extend the text should not be lost. For example, where a short piece of text is accompanied by an illustration the narrator might choose to discuss the picture in more detail, give anecdotes, suggest further sources of reference or direct the child, if he so wishes, to fast-forward to a particular counter number (or mark on the cassette window) or collect another coded cassette tape where more recorded information is to be found. However, where the tape and the text part company needs to be made clear in order to avoid confusion, and complete red herrings are to be avoided at any cost.

Fifth, we should never underestimate the potential of teachers as frustrated actors. With a little encouragement colleagues are only too willing to co-operate in the making of the tapes, happy to record a brief moment of fame in a resource pack for future generations of children to enjoy. The recording sessions can be great fun and the more experienced one becomes the greater the temptation to be adventurous and to experiment further with the medium. The drama department can be a treasure trove of narrators and actors, using different voices, sound effects and so on. Perhaps the music department would like to contribute some atmospheric background or foreground. The more rich and varied the audio experience and the more enthusiastic the participants, the greater the responsiveness and enthusiasm of the children for whom the conventional written text is a source of monotony and boredom.

Sixth, the exercises and questions themselves need to be recorded on the cassette. Nothing could be more of a let-down after a stimulating audio experience than being thrown back to the printed text unsoftened by other media.

Finally, the fifth R need not be a solitary experience for the child. While there are technical problems in linking up systems with junction-boxes and multiple headphones, the sharing of the activities has something to commend it. Of course, the complete independence of each participant is lost, and for most purposes individual recorders are to be preferred. Schools cannot easily stretch the finances to provide the full facilities, but given the current vogue for the personal stereo (Walkman) some youngsters will be easily encouraged to bring their own sets from home. Caution will be necessary – the probability of unauthorised use of sets in other people's lessons is high as, in many schools, is the probability of theft. (It is also advisable to check from time to time that it *is* the approved cassette they are listening to and not the latest release from a leading pop group!)

Clearly, the possibilities of the fifth R as a substitute for or supplement to the conventional worksheet are considerable. The ability of the child to work at his/her own pace without making calls on the teacher to repeat or explain some word/sentence/passage, and the sheer satisfaction of having the control of learning firmly in one's own hands make this a valuable ingredient of the resource package. But to see it as simply a more interesting or alternative medium for the acquisition of knowledge would be short-sighted; there are clearly considerable implications also for the development of creative and expressive activities in which the child is far from being a passive recipient of existing knowledge.

From tape to text: the active role Even in the composition of answers to apparently 'closed' questions, the recorder may facilitate a surprisingly creative response. But instruction needs to be given not only on the simple operations of the record button, but also on how to delete a section, pause for thought, 'overwrite' a section and, finally, edit the final copy. Children can learn a lot through experimenting to discover the best way of ordering ideas and then transferring them to magnetic tape. Finally, thought must be given to ways and means of transferring the taped response to paper.

However, it is in the more open, free or expressive work that the machine as a tool for the creator comes into its own. Consider, for example the following two extracts from the work of the same twelve-year-old child. The first (describing a book read by the child at home) is a piece of free written expression, which clearly betrays his difficulties with using a very limited spelling vocabulary. The second, composed in response to a lesson where part of the stimulus was the poem *Flannan Isle*, is transcribed (with minimal editing) from a cassette recording produced by the same boy only a few weeks later.

Extract 1

Free written expression   Mr Lazy

1. Mr Lazy Sleep all day

2. Mr Lazy drams of ben a Sleep

3. The house work never gets dun

4. His favourite Place is bed

5. and ever Thing he dose slowley

Extract 2

Transcribed from cassette

The Flannan Island Story
Starring: Peter and Paul.

One day Peter was looking in the newspaper.

'Oy, Paul, look in this newspaper. It says a job for Flannan Island lighthouse. Let's go and apply for that job.'

Peter and Paul go off to the newspaper office to ask about the job.

'Have you come for a job in the newspaper?' asked Bob, the newspaper reporter. 'Which one do you want?'

'The Flannan lighthouse job,' replied Paul.

'Well, you can have it,' said Bob.

'Why are you that desperate to get someone for it?' asked Peter. 'Never mind, we'll take the job.'

'How much do you pay?' asked Paul. Bob explained that they would get £200 each a month, but they would get all their food free and the electricity and heating.

Peter wanted to know how often they would get their food and mail, and Bob said that it would be once a week.

'How do we get over to the island?' enquired Paul.

'There's a slight problem there,' said Bob. 'You have to supply your own boat.'

'Why?' they wanted to know.

'Never mind,' said Paul. 'We can use my speed-boat.'

Bob was rather relieved that he didn't have to explain about the missing boat and people

Peter was a bit worried because he might get sea-sick, but Paul told him it was a short trip and not to panic.

Peter and Paul said goodbye and thanked the reporter for the job. They decided to go for a drink at the *Cross Keys*.

'Two pints of bitter,' asked Peter. The barman was reading the newspaper.

'Who'd ever reply for this job on Flannan Island?' wondered the barman.

Paul answered, 'Peter and I have.'

'You didn't, did you?' asked the barman.

Paul said, 'Oh, yes, we did.'

The barman shook his head and told them about the strange goings-on up on Flannan Island. Paul thought that he was only joking. But the barman went on to tell them about the three men who had gone missing and the appearance of three mysterious, black, ugly birds.

'It sounds really weird,' said Paul.

'I wish we hadn't taken the job, added Peter.

'Never mind, everything will be okay. We'll look after ourselves,' said Paul bravely. 'I know you are a bit of a coward, Peter, but we have accepted the job already. We can go for a couple of days and if it is all right we can carry on.'

Peter murmured, 'What if we see a ghost or witch?'

Paul was unsure but nevertheless he said that there were no ghosts or witches. 'We won't see anything,' he said.

After their drink at the *Cross Keys*, Peter and Paul left in the speed-boat for Flannan Island and the lighthouse. On the way Peter was sick over the side of the boat. Peter managed to say, 'Thanks a lot for talking me into it.'

'Shut up,' replied Paul.

'It's easy for you to say. You don't get sea-sick,' said Peter. He was very glad to reach Flannan Island. 'Land at last,' he said.

Paul took charge and told Peter to go and unlock the lighthouse while he tied up the boat. Peter was very scared and said no, so Paul said that he would go and open the lighthouse and put on the lights while he left Peter to tie up the boat. But Peter would not do that either. He didn't want to be left by himself. So in the end they both tied up the boat and went to unlock the door together.

Peter was very frightened and kept imagining that someone was going to grab him. Paul turned on the lights and Peter locked the door behind them once they were inside.

'Nobody's in here, said Paul. He looked around and found that food had been left untouched on the table.

'Did you put that food on the table?' he asked Peter.

'No,' replied Peter.

'How very strange,' said Paul. 'Come on, chicken,' he added.

'Chicken I may be, but I'd rather eat bird seed than go in there,' said Peter.

Just then a seagull flew over, screeching. Peter rushed after Paul, 'I'm coming,' he shouted. 'Wait for me, boy.'

Paul continued looking round and noticed a chair had been knocked over. A seagull screeched past again.

'He must be hungry,' said Paul. 'We might as well sit down and eat.'

'I'm not eating that food, it might have something in it. It might be contaminated,' worried Peter.

They decided to go and light the lighthouse lamp. It was a long way up to the top. Peter thought he could hear someone behind them but he noticed that it was his knees knocking. Paul enjoyed the lovely view from the top of the lighthouse, but Peter wondered what it would be like at night-time if the three birds flew past.

When they went down to the sleeping quarters the light went on by itself. Peter thought it was ghosts but Paul thought it was the bird.

Just then they heard a flapping noise and screeching and saw the three ugly birds the barman had told them about. It was then that they noticed a man lying dead on the rocks below.

Peter was worried that the man would jump out on them but Paul told him not to be silly, as he was dead. When they went outside the birds flew around them and they saw their ugly faces. As it was getting late they decided to leave the man and go to bed. They spent a restless night imagining all sorts of horrible things.

The next day they did some cleaning, dusting and polishing. While they were doing the windows the three black ugly birds flew back screeching, and flapping their wings. Peter was scared. They chased him to the top of the lighthouse.

'What's that noise? They're coming after me,' he shouted as he ran up the stairs. At the top he backed against a window and the birds come at him and with a horrible yell he fell to the rocks below – dead.

Paul went to see where Peter was...

The difference speaks for itself! Freeing him from the burden of writing has had a dramatic effect on the quality of this child's work. The story was transcribed, typed and then shown to the child. The incredulity and delight in his voice cannot properly be appreciated from the written words alone: 'Did *I* do *that!*'. The effect of this on his self-image and the kudos which resulted is difficult to measure, but he must have received a considerable boost from such an achievement. Certainly many of his teachers expressed amazement at the quality of the story, and whatever the personal satisfaction gained, a more positive and more *accurate* perception of this child's talents was one major outcome.

To accept the tape itself as a medium by which a satisfactory piece of written work might be composed, let alone as an alternative final form for such work, is something schools and examination boards have been curiously reluctant to do. Valuing the written word above all else – or simply through a blinkered and indolent conservatism – they have yet to recognise the incredible potential of such a commonplace alternative. Yet if we seek excellence for all, we must provide *every* opportunity for the child to exploit the potential of the learning environment. Surely the fifth R is a rich provider of just such opportunities?

3 The implications for lesson involvement If the resource pack is limited to conventional tasks in the cognitive-intellectual domain, then we have not progressed very far. The aesthetic-artistic, physical-manual and social-interpersonal are equally important areas of the curriculum and we suggest that they should not be completely isolated in separate specialist subjects (art, CDT, PSE and so on). Rather, these should be equally the target of other parts of the curriculum where, we would argue, they are not only developed in their own right, but throw up a considerable range of alternative teaching-learning experiences by which the academic curriculum may be explored.

This idea is not new. It was a central principle in the Charity James/ Goldsmiths College development of IDE/M – (interdisciplinary enquiry/making) (C James, 1968). Education requires that children be provided with choices of means for exploring and expressing a particular theme through a combination of media comfortable to them. The possibilities are infinite, but although many primary schools flourish by challenging children to explore and respond in ways other than the written word, secondary schools have hardly moved.

This is not the place to describe at length the whole gamut of progressive teaching methods and expressive/creative learning activities, but we would suggest that the resource package should include, require, or be accompanied by opportunities for such diverse activities as:

drama
role-play
games – from computer simulations to board-game variants on monopoly, snakes-and-ladders and jigsaws
graphs and chart-work (pie-charts, column and bar graphs; histograms, etc)
painting and photography
sketching
model-making (including the utilisation of commercial kits such as Lego and Meccano)
puppetry
origami
poetry
collage
posters
cartoons
murals
friezes
word-processing and 'read-back' speech packages
computer-graphics
music
dance
interviewing and survey-work
Cuisenaire rods and Dienes blocks, etc

Nor should the traditional *individualism* of the curriculum be lightly endorsed. Many items in the above list entail group activities and team-work and this is, in our view, essential to balance the emphasis on independent work in the central pamphlet.

Finally, we must not forget the importance of *talk*. For over a decade Tough (1976), Barnes et al (1971) and others have been pointing out the virtues of engaging children in the variety of talk from which learning springs, and the American radicals Postman and Weingartner (1971) have advocated 'languaging' as *the* medium by which learning is effected. Debate, discussion, dialogue, exposition and exegesis are not the prerogative of academics: they are the stuff of effective communication at all levels and ought to be practised and employed in our teaching to a much greater extent.

Now notice how our discussion of resource packs and how they might be so organised as to facilitate the education of those who encounter learning difficulties has led into a general appeal for a curriculum and a pedagogy which is more open and more varied. What children with 'special needs' so often require is not something radically different from 'other' children, since *all* children experience difficulties of one sort or another, but simply what *all* children need: a better and more vigorous curriculum pursued through a more varied and enlightened pedagogy. None the less, specific needs require specific responses, and in Rickstones School it has been found necessary to complement a general commitment to integration with a system of short-term workshops.

The workshop

Workshops provide a method for making in-roads into the area of special needs without rigid and debilitating labels. They are by no means limited to the traditional areas of 'weakness' – reading, writing and numeracy – but include, for example, graphical skills, extension work, measuring and comprehension, and this means that even the most talented child may take part, as, for example, in the case of someone with particularly poor handwriting.

Although a room has been prepared with individual work carrels and stocked with teaching machines, language consoles, cassette-recorders, reading schemes, problem-solving materials, spelling programmes, numeracy games, sets of comprehension exercises, extension work and so on, it is not necessarily here that the most important work takes place. Much work can be, and is, done in the classroom setting, where programmes of work are monitored and extended without an obvious break in the particular lesson, and, of course, exercises to be done at home also play an important role.

To minimise disruption in the child's classroom work, the workshop session itself runs for no more than fifteen minutes, with children leaving their normal classroom to discuss their progress and collect the next instalment of material aimed at developing a specific skill. Obviously, these arrangements are not made on an *ad hoc* basis and negotiation has to take place between class teacher and support teacher to agree the most suitable and convenient times for children to attend these short sessions. Once a timetable has been agreed and printed the onus rests with the child to keep the appointments. For the children this is rarely a problem and they are quick to remind their class teacher regularly of the commitment they have made to attend a session.

Crucial to the success of the workshop is its voluntary nature. No one is forced to attend a workshop, and where difficulties have arisen these have been resolved by delicate negotiation to find a compromise which satisfies all parties. In the final analysis, it is better that children make their own decisions and perhaps change their minds later than insist they submit to the school's demands. Children are not fools and, if they can see benefits to be derived from a particular activity, they are keen to get involved. In our experience it is the children who are the ambassadors for this system and it is they who sell the workshop session to their peers, setting in motion a sort of inflation: the more children seek this scarce commodity of individual skills-development, the greater becomes its value in the eyes of potential consumers. To date, both pupils and teachers have received the system well.

Workshop groups change in membership according to the changing focus of assistance – those who need help with graph work are not necessarily poor spellers – but also according to the scale of the individual's need and rate of progress. Some will attend for just the odd session while others will develop a regular long-term involvement. However, no more than six children are seen at one time, and no child attends more than three workshops in any one week. The latter is a necessary restriction, since a weekly involvement of longer than forty-five minutes would seriously affect the continuity of class-room experience. There is also the possibility that children will exploit the system as an excuse for ducking out of the lesson for a few minutes, rather than as an opportunity to develop a valuable skill, so some limits are desirable.

Regardless of the number of workshops children attend, detailed records are kept to monitor the progress they make on the defined objectives agreed at the commencement of a programme. Some programmes contain assessment forms which allow children, parents, class teachers and support teachers to comment on the child's work and make recommendations for further consid-eration. An abridged example of such a form is given in Figure 9. This monitoring demonstrates for all concerned the value being attached to the child's progress through the programme and has a significant effect in prom-oting the image of the workshop. It also signifies the importance given to the system's response to individual needs, as assessed from different points of view, and is an approach which has scope for extension in other workshop and lesson activities.

Figure 9

SECTION 1

Do you think this course has helped you to improve:

		Student YES NO			Student YES NO	
Your	thinking			research skills		
	presentation			oral work		
	written work			spelling		
	handwriting			reading		
	initiative			motivation		
	effort			....		
	....			....		

Was this work new to you?   YES/NO

SECTION 2

Have you found the work:

challenging		too much	
stimulating		useful	
difficult		useless	
easy		....	

Which section of the work did you find most interesting and why?

....

Is there a section of the work you did not enjoy and why?

....

What further improvements could you make to your work?

....

Do you wish to continue with the course?   YES/NO

SECTION 3

Is there any other skill/activity you would like to develop?

....

Have you any other comments to make?

....

Would your parents like to make any comments?

....

Would your tutor like to make any comments?
....

Would subject teachers like to make any comments?

....

Support Teacher   ....

....

The modular curriculum

In Rickstones school the main thrust of the school's special needs policy has been the integration of academic support into the normal routine of the classroom subject-lesson built around pamphlets and related resource packages, and supplemented by workshop-focused programmes of individual skills-support. However, it is arguable that the problem of the appeal of the curriculum to all children requires a more fundamental restructuring of what we offer. In particular, the conventional situation in which children in the final two years are often forced to take a diet of grammar school subjects (assessed either annually or in one fell swoop at the end), based on a dubious understanding of what is involved in them, is simply unacceptable. As Hamblin (1978) points out, this commitment at the age of fourteen to a two-year programme comes at a time when the youngster is likely to have a good many other pressures upon his/her shoulders, and a wrong decision can only lead to waning enthusiasm, deep disaffection and (at worst) open rejection at a later date. Careful counselling accompanied by sessions of group guidance to consider the complexities of the choice to be made – and, indeed, to explore the very process of such decision-making – may minimise the traumas involved, but it is arguable that a different style of curriculum programme is what is really needed. The idea of a *modular curriculum* has grown out of such concerns.

Ideally, the modular curriculum provides a range of relatively small and discrete units or modules of work from which children may choose combinations, permitting variety both of content and order. The main advantages for such an approach would seem to lie in its flexibility and capacity to develop programmes of work to meet individual needs, coupled with short-term goals continually assessed throughout (for example) the half-term duration of each module. This avoids the pressures of long-term deferred gratification traditionally associated with the one- or two-year examination courses. There is an opportunity here to develop assessment procedures which focus attention on skills and learning processes rather than solely on the transmission of subject knowledge. The inherent strengths are spelled out in the ILEA's report under the chairmanship of David Hargreaves (1984) entitled *Improving Secondary Schools*, and include: readily defined and perceived purpose, content and method of recording; negotiated means by which the unit's goals can be reached; the appeal of shorter-term objectives to all students; and a unit credit giving a tangible assessment which is jointly agreed to evaluate the extent to which unit objectives have been achieved (p74).

Rickstones School has, for a number of years, run a limited pilot scheme to assess the potential of a similar programme. The school places great store in personal and social education with every fourth- and fifth-year child embarking on a course called Life Studies, the centre-piece of which is the two-week work experience element for all fifth-year pupils. The modular course is an optional off-shoot from Life Studies and contains half-termly components including: education for parenthood, consumer education, information technology, recreational pursuits, home skills (adventurous cooking, cooking for one), media studies, driving course and DIY (plumbing, electrics, routine household jobs and maintenance).

The practical nature of the course must be stressed, with group work and role play taking precedence over textbook learning. In its first year of operation the course was oversubscribed and, to limit the number of pupils to approximately eighteen per module, additional staff and courses had to be arranged. Falling rolls have meant that this figure has now crept up to twenty pupils per module and what was once envisaged as a course catering for the needs of a small group of pupils has grown to provide a service for upwards of one-third of all fourth- and fifth-year pupils.

Summary

In this chapter we have attempted to shift the focus of academic and pastoral support away from the emotional and cognitive first aid to which it so often reduces. We have argued that supportive education requires to be proactive and that this entails provision for individual needs through an approach to opening the curriculum to all children.

There is nothing new in much of what we have said: resource-based learning, the need for study, library and other information-handling skills, the promise of systematic and sensible tutorial programmes, and the independent learning of the thematic worksheet/pamphlet/folder have all had their advocates and their practitioners down the years. Even the modular curriculum is by no means unheard of in different degrees and under a variety of names. But schools have not, by and large, been very adventurous in their policies for change along these lines.

While it is unfashionable to say so in official quarters, we believe it is time for education to take on a new face, where the supremacy of learning and recording facts in writing is tempered by a sincere encouragement of freedom of expression; in which children negotiate and use the most comfortable means at their disposal for obtaining access to the curriculum; and in which schools make the children aware of alternative channels for communication in such a way as to avoid any suggestion that they are a second-rate substitute for real education. To illustrate how this might be achieved we have used the efforts of one school which, while by no means perfect, has certainly done more than many to open the curriculum to all. We believe other schools must address the whole curriculum issue afresh, with the implications of the integration of academic and pastoral support firmly on the agenda.

To do this requires a receptiveness and inventiveness hitherto unheard of in many schools. Unreflective acceptance of 'the way we've always done it' is the bane of progress, so a move towards what we have called *supportive education* will inevitably involve the re-education of staff and the development both of new skills and new perspectives. The raising of staff awareness of the potential of alternatives, and the means by which appropriate skills might be developed, is the focus of the next chapter.

7 Raising teacher awareness: a break with tradition

Throughout this book we have been critical of conventional ideas about the nature of the problems which the concept of special needs often describes, and of the traditional structures and practices for dealing with them. In a more positive vein, we have described and exemplified an alternative approach – supportive education – which is designed to integrate academic and pastoral support in ways which will be both more effective educationally and more acceptable (and successful) on social and moral grounds.

The promotion of such alternatives is an invitation to schools to make quite radical changes to their organisation and practices. It also implies a break with traditional ideas and attitudes, some of which are likely to be deeply entrenched in the minds and routines of school staff. Attempts to change structure and practice are unlikely to meet with success if those who have to make those changes work are not thinking in appropriate ways or hold attitudes which are incompatible with, or even antagonistic towards, what is being proposed. Nicholls has summarised the conditions which are likely to lead to the successful implementation of 'a complex educational innovation in a comprehensive school':

'1 There should be a clear understanding of the innovation.
2 The teachers should have the necessary knowledge of planning processes and the skills and abilities to develop and carry out the innovation.
3 Criteria for the evaluation of the innovation should be stated in advance.
4 Account should be taken of resistance to the innovation when it is identified.
5 There should be knowledge of and attention given to the process of implementing the innovation.'
(Nicholls, *Managing Educational Innovations*, 1983, pp48–49)

In a sense, the changing of *minds* is a necessary prerequisite for successful changes in the organisation, but this does not mean that it must be *temporally* prior. Indeed, it is arguable that one effective way of changing attitudes is to involve people in the planning and implementation of particular innovations: in making structural and procedural changes, those involved may well experience changes of attitude more or less as a matter of course. However that may be, for many teachers, change requires a raising of awareness of the nature of their daily activities and a measure of re-education about what it is that they ought to be doing.

To some extent teachers and headteachers should be more receptive to proposals for change than they have been in the past. Work like that of Rutter et al (1979) has tried to correct the impression that failures in learning and social adjustment are always the product of within-child factors or of home circumstances, and has given a nudge to the complacency of those teachers who imagine that their schools are above criticism. Moreover, there has been a growing demand for more systematic evaluation and appraisal in schools generally, not unconnected with the present government's commitment to greater accountability. At the time of writing, legislation to facilitate some form of compulsory teacher appraisal is promised in the next session of Parliament, and the secretary of state has repeatedly taken steps to improve the productivity of schools by requiring stronger local authority and national control over the curriculum.

Elsewhere, bodies like the School Curriculum Development Committee have taken (and supported) initiatives in in-school evaluation and innovation, with the *Guideline for Review and Internal Development in Schools* (GRIDS) being perhaps the best known. Finally, changes in policy and practice where the integration of children with special needs are concerned have done something to heighten teachers' awareness of the problems and possibilities of change in this area. In this context the *named person* policy, in which specific individuals are charged with a responsibility for promoting and highlighting the cause of special needs provision, has provided schools with another catalyst for change.

However, it would be wrong to imagine that every school and every teacher is equally ready to countenance fundamental changes in either their perceptions of educational need or their own practices. Despite repeated claims that the majority of learning difficulties arise from the inappropriateness of the ordinary curriculum, the forces which resist change often come from within the school and are fuelled by the conservative values of the very people who, ironically, are advocating evaluation and appraisal. In any case, there is a human factor whose significance is not to be underestimated. It must be appreciated that whenever there is the possibility of change it is accompanied by a sense of anxiety on the part of those most directly involved. This anxiety is felt by both subject teacher and special needs teacher alike and must be handled with sensitivity if we are to provide a feeling of security and sense of direction during the period of transition.

Clearly, then, issues in the management of change and innovation cannot be divorced from the problem of winning over those teachers who are going to implement any change. But there is a further factor which is crucial, because it is, as it were, at the forefront of any initiative, and that is the know-how, abilities and, above all, *skills* of the teachers involved. It is not enough to be aware of the need for change: one also needs to be equipped with a repertoire of skills and strategies for carrying out the day-to-day business of teaching within a reformed system.

It is the purpose of this chapter to consider these issues and to suggest ways in which headteachers and their staffs might more effectively plan and implement change through the management of innovation and the development of staff expertise through a variety of INSET activities. As in previous chapters, we will not attempt to prescribe a set of hard and fast procedures for every school to follow, since what is appropriate for one school may not be appropriate for others. Rather, we shall discuss some general principles and suggest a number of models which might inform any programme for change, and then indicate some possible activities which might lead to the achievement of objectives.

The nature of change

Change in educational organisations is normal. Despite the fact that the conventional subject curriculum and the procedures of the secondary school day often seem little different from those of twenty or thirty years ago – we still teach science, art, mathematics, English, etc, in periods which begin and end with the bell – changes of greater or lesser magnitude are happening all the time. New subjects appear, old ones are reorganised or integrated, variations are made in the length and organisation of the school day, uniforms come and go, new examinations (e.g. GCSE) appear, pastoral systems are simplified – or complicated (see Best *et al*, 1983), technological innovations (AVA, micros, school broadcasting, etc) gradually find their way into schools, SCDC projects are implemented, LEA advisors ring the changes in pedagogy and content, and so on. Some of these changes are *endogenous* – deriving from the internal workings of the school as a closed system – while others are *exogenous* – deriving from, and sometimes imposed by, external bodies. Some change is therefore upon the initiative of the school staff; other change is a response by the school to outside pressures. At any point in time, a school will be subject to a mixture of changes which are partly endogenous and partly exogenous, and in which staff are at times being *proactive* and at other times *reactive*. This is obviously true of change in the area of supportive education, in which school initiatives are set in a pattern of responses required by outside bodies and sometimes triggered by political events.

It is also possible to categorise educational change in terms of the likelihood of success or failure of any initiative. Holmes (1986) has distinguished between *high risk* and *low risk* changes. The former are initiatives in which, for one or more reasons, there is a relatively poor chance of success and at worst the prospect of a backlash of reaction, which, far from achieving desired reforms, culminates in retrogressive change. Low risk changes are pursued in areas in which, for various reasons, the chances of success are good, and in which there are probably by-products in the form of other equally welcome innovations. The risks involved in seeking change have to be balanced against the potential gains to be made: we may be willing to risk a very great deal if the prize is a pearl of great price, but unwilling to gamble with what is meritorious in the status quo if the potential gains are marginal. We may think of programmes for change as being one of the following four types:

high risk and high gain
low risk but high gain
high risk but low gain
low risk and low gain

It would be nice if all educational innovation was of the second kind, but, alas, it is not so. The kinds of change we are advocating are of the first kind – high risk but high gain. The prize is of great value, for it is nothing less than the provision of a proper education for a section of the school population which is currently (and traditionally) losing out in all sorts of ways: by being offered a poorly taught, irrelevant and watered-down curriculum, dominated by the three Rs and/or a system of oppressive 'care', all within a set of structural arrangements that are segregationist, stigmatising, divisive, alienating and fundamentally inegalitarian. All members of the school population will be the beneficiaries of the integrated provision of academic and pastoral support we are advocating.

However, the risk of failure is considerable for a number of related reasons. First, the notion of supportive education challenges the current value system of our schools, and the assumptions made about the nature of education, educability and need. Second, it seeks to change teachers' attitudes to their work and to the relative importance of the various roles they have to play in school. The high status traditionally attached to teaching academic subjects to high-ability children is threatened by the recognition of the crucial importance of the expert advisory service which supportive staff may perform for them. Third, it raises resource and timetabling issues – what rooms are needed and what arrangement of physical space is required for an integrated approach, how can a 'floater' be timetabled supernumerary to the subject teachers at any time, where is the money to come from for cassettes, furniture and all the other hard- and soft-ware which a child-centred approach necessitates, and so on? Fourth, by virtue of its apparent concern with those children who are traditionally conceived of as having low status, and its involvement with the pastoral care of children (rather than the strictly academic development of the pupil) it is going to be difficult to promote in competition with the interests (often entrenched) of the academic curriculum and those who specialise in it. Finally, innovations inevitably involve extra work for teachers, and this is not always welcomed. As Nicholls (1983) comments:

'Some teachers find participation in innovation so stimulating and exciting that they willingly accept the extra work; others might accept the extra work for other reasons: they might, for instance, see involvement in innovation as a way of promotion. There are other teachers, however, less enthusiastic about innovation or perhaps deriving their professional satisfaction from their class-room activities, who are much less willing to take on the additional task of innovating.' (pp4–5)

To achieve change in the face of these difficulties is clearly going to require not only the political will of management and their allies, but eventually the *corporate* will of the staff of the school as a whole – and, arguably, of the children and their parents. In the first instance, there is a need for those seeking change to win as many allies to their cause as possible.

A model of management strategy

In a short but interesting article Graham Peeke (1984) develops the following *Typology of Teacher Responses to Innovation*:

'*The Diehards* are fervently conservative and resistant to change of any nature.

The Loyalists are committed to existing practice and are unwilling to transfer their loyalties from an existing curriculum to a new one. Such a stance may be rationalised by criticising the innovation on such grounds as lack of planning, inadequate preparation or cost.

The Diffidents. Such teachers are self-effacing, proclaiming a willingness to adopt an innovation, but a willingness which is hindered by a lack of necessary knowledge and/or skills.

The Pragmatists may also maintain a willingness to adopt an innovation, but their enthusiasm is tempered by a negative evaluation of the practical consequences. During implementation, such teachers may discover difficulties which were unforseen before the new curriculum was put into practice.

The Ideologues are adherents of an ideology which conflicts with the ideology of the innovation. Often such conflicts do not become clearly apparent until implementation is attempted. Because of this, these teachers may initially declare themselves, at least conditionally, in favour of the innovation.

The Mitigators are favourably inclined towards the innovation, but are concerned to modify some of its features, particularly the content, which they may see as inappropriate to the needs of their specific students.

The Advocates speak in favour of the innovation and may be either progressive or uncritical.' (p23)

According to this model, the innovator can expect a range of responses to any proposal, with negative responses from the diehards and loyalists, conditional responses from the diffidents, pragmatists and ideologues, and positive responses from the mitigators and advocates.

These three broad categories correspond to those of the radical, the uncommitted and the conservative in a model offered by Best et al (*Education and Care* 1983. pp216–223), relating them to the degree of power or authority which individual teachers enjoy. Using Weber's (R Aron, *Main Currents in Sociological Thought*, Vol 2, 1968, pp240–243) typology of 'legal-rational', 'traditional' and 'charismatic' authority, they suggest that teachers can be seen as 'influential', 'marginal' or 'impotent' when it comes to affecting the course of any proposed innovation. It is not simply whether a particular teacher responds positively (or negatively, or conditionally) that is important, but also whether he/she is in a position of influence. Influential radicals are the innovator's best allies, influential conservatives the innovator's worst enemies. As Lawrence and Lorsch (1969) observe:

'While an organisation can afford to have some members who will comply with the new requirements with but faint enthusiasm and a very few who are in active opposition, most of the key figures need both understanding and emotional commitment if important and lasting change is to be effected.'
(Quoted in Best *et al*, *Education and Care*, 1983, p221)

The problem has two elements to it: first, how to redistribute power and influence so as to increase the 'clout' of allies who are currently impotent or marginal, whilst decreasing the power of currently influential enemies; second, to win the battle for the understanding and emotional commitment of those key figures who are currently uncommitted or whose response (for one reason or another) has been no more than conditional.

This may be achieved by a variety of strategies. Following Chin and Benn (1974), Best *et al* (1983) distinguish between three types of strategy:

'1 *Empirical-rational* strategies which involve demonstrating to members that a particular situation or procedure makes sense under the circumstances, and is in any case in members' own interests;

2 *Normative-re-educative* strategies in which socio-cultural values are invoked to legitimate a situation or course of action in order to gain members' commitment to it. Appeals to wider values and

ideals and an affective as well as rational response are characteristics of such strategies;

3 *Power-coercive* strategies in which the compliance of those with less power to the plans of those with greater power is achieved by more or less naked, more or less manipulative, direction or leadership from above.'

(Best *et al*, 1983, pp220–221)

In bringing about any complex innovation probably some combination of these strategies will be necessary. Obviously, the more that can be achieved by a normative re-educative approach the better. For one thing, this involves the innovator in justifying his or her proposal on moral grounds, thus providding some hard test of its theoretical desirability. More importantly, perhaps, like all genuine converts, those who are swayed by appeals to their deepest values are going to be more committed than those who are simply bribed or coerced into accepting the change.

There is a point, however, at which stern measures may have to be taken. Influential diehards or entrenched loyalists may refuse to succumb to even the most eloquently argued and morally sound case, at which point the innovators must either force compliance or remove the culprits from positions of influence. Thus, for example, the study by Best *et al* (1983) of the styles of three headteachers in 'Rivendell' recalls how one head neutralised an opponent by putting her in charge of the library, a notorious backwater from which she was in a poor position even to know what was happening, let alone affect the course of events.

Anyone wishing to change significantly the organisation of special needs education, must recognise the variety of responses with which their initiative is likely to be met, and to appreciate that the whole thing is very much a *political* phenomenon. Some careful weighing-up of potential opposition to change is essential, as is some strategy for overcoming it.

Innovation by consensus

The foregoing discussion will not have pleased everyone. Those who like to think that teachers and educational administrators are entirely honourable will have found the model unduly manipulative and cynical. However, we suggest that much of the micro-politics of schooling is precisely as described in the model, and that it would be folly to pretend otherwise. Of course, the most acceptable (and most effective) form of winning allies and redistributing influence and authority will be by winning the support of staff through sound argument and through achieving a consensus about desirable objectives and the means for their attainment. This seems especially important where initiatives to do with care, support and concern are involved, since the medium is the message and any scheme aimed to increase equality, justice and respect for persons is hardly likely to appeal if it is imposed in a ruthless or manipulative way. *The wide and thorough discussion and exploration of possibilities by as many people as possible is a necessary ingredient in any successful programme for introducing supportive education.*

Such discussion need not always involve every member of staff in some kind of grand forum – indeed, small 'buzz groups' or workshops might be more successful, especially if they are each given clear terms of reference and a clear focus for their deliberations. However this is handled, we can suggest a number of key questions that need to be addressed:

1 Do we *need* to change our provision for the support of both learning and the child as a person? How do we know whether we need change? Have we evaluated our existing arrangements? If so, what implications do the findings have for a model of supportive education? If not, how should we now proceed to make such an evaluation?

2 Do we *want* change in supportive education? Do we *all* want it? If not, who does and who doesn't and why? Can we identify reasons, motives or interests behind these attitudes? Can we share our feelings about change? Do we feel threatened, stimulated, excited or bored by it? How can it be made more acceptable?

3 What needs to be changed?

a Teacher-*practices* – pedagogy, guidance, counselling, class-room organisation, planning, etc?
b Supportive *processes* – e.g. communications, record-keeping?
c Organisational *structures* – role definitions, job descriptions, the bureaucracy itself, committee structures, formal procedures, institutionalised routines?
d The *curriculum* – does it require opening/support/reform/re-styling/augmenting?
e Teacher-*attitudes* – are teacher perspectives compatible with/accommodating to supportive education?

4 What is the *scale* of the change required? Is a major across-the-curriculum or whole-school policy envisaged or is some piecemeal, incremental change appropriate? Is it closer to revolutionary change or gradual reform? Is the scale of change needed likely to be feasible?

5 What should be the *rate* of change? Can this be accomplished in the short, medium or long term? Can some objectives be achieved more quickly than others? Is there an absolute limit to the pace of change? Will staff experience something like Toffler's (1970) 'future shock' or, on the contrary, lose interest if it doesn't happen overnight?

6 What *resources* will be needed? What are the likely requirements in terms of money, hardware, software, facilities, rooms, storage space and access to other parts of the institution? What competing demands are there for these resources? Most importantly, where is the person-power and the time to come

from in a staff which already feels stretched? How might existing resources be released to facilitate the programme?

7 What are the *implications* of the change *for other parts of the system*? Change is never entirely discrete or self-contained: there is inevitably a knock-on effect of greater or lesser proportions. A change in any of the areas in 3 above inevitably affects one or more of the others. Here we would emphasise two additional considerations:

a What effect will the change have on the individual's self-image and professional status; what is the personal cost of the innovation to those who are involved in it, and how is this likely to affect their attitudes to the change?
b Given that a knock-on effect is inevitable, how can responsibility for the stream of changes be determined; what is the impact on existing patterns of *accountability*?

8 What *staff development* will be needed to facilitate change and make the innovation work? As well as the education of staff about the change itself and the need to win their support for what is proposed, what specific skills will be required of staff? These will include skills of person management, curriculum planning, observation, evaluation, resource management and so on, but they will also include specific *pedagogic* skills, such as group-work with adolescents (see Button, 1974), counselling, preparation and presentation of alternative learning materials, techniques for one-to-one tutorials and small-group workshops, the use of drama, etc.

Of course these various considerations have been presented here in a fairly general way, since the requirements of each particular school and each particular innovation will be different. However, we suggest that those beginning to plan a development towards supportive education will find the foregoing a useful notional agenda to give direction to their efforts.

INSET and staff development

Obviously, much of the previous section has been about staff development and this raises the whole question of what is an appropriate form of in-service education and training for the kinds of reform we have in mind. Given the nature and possible broad scale of the innovation, and given that it is confined to the unique situation of your school, we suggest that INSET should be corporate, extended and with space for extreme views to be advanced. Because supportive education requires integration of supportive specialists and their services into the mainstream of the curriculum, there is a need to adopt a whole-school or corporate perspective, at least in the early stages. Since the proposals are at the level of fundamental philosophies and teacher attitudes – not easy to change by any means – this process is clearly going to take time. And since supportive education challenges orthodox practice and the entrenched values upon which it is based, discussion is bound to generate some heat: this cannot be ignored, but extreme positions need to be presented and opened up for debate. You will never get everyone to agree with everything you wish to initiate, nor should you; for the innovators need to be receptive to constructive criticism of their developing programme, and in the fullness of time a respectful agreement by some members to differ on some aspects of the plan will be as much as can be hoped for, and is to be much preferred to an ill-considered and ill-informed showdown, with half the staff walking out in high dudgeon.

In the early stages, staff need opportunities to benefit from the wisdom of others. No one wants to re-invent the wheel if they can help it. Arranging a series of *seminars* in which specific members lead a discussion of recent literature in the field – HMI reports, journal articles (from, for example, *Remedial Education* or *Pastoral Care in Education*), specific chapters from books – is one way of informing practice with thought and reflection right from the start. This might well be linked to the convening of teacher support groups for the discussion of particular children and particular problems. In this respect, Hanko (1985) advocates the use of a consultant to guide discussions in which teachers from within the same school or from a number of neighbouring schools, share in the exploration of strategies for responding to problems of both learning and adjustment.

Arranging for staff to undertake fact-finding missions to other schools where inspiring examples of good practice can be observed, followed by a report-back that highlights the relative applicability to one's own school in terms of the similarities and differences which obtain, is also worth doing. During the discussion, the specifics of change in one's own institution will begin to emerge, including the precise skills which will need to be developed in individuals later.

Against this background of widening corporate awareness – and, hopefully, commitment to development – *task-groups* can be set up to explore in detail aspects of the situation and of the emerging pattern of change. One group may be concerned with producing a *schedule for change*. What is the appropriate order and time-scale for the innovation? Are some things necessary prerequisites for others to happen? Will some things be sufficient to set in motion a train of other desirable events, or does the whole series of events need timetabling? Another group may be asked to undertake a *costing* exercise, not merely (or primarily) in terms of the money involved, but rather in terms of all those negative effects which may be unavoidable, at least in the short run. Many such costs can be anticipated in general terms by the questions posed on pages 114-115. For example, what is the likely cost in terms of goodwill on the part of staff whose professional status and self-image is affected? How disruptive to other (currently satisfactory) aspects of the school is the innovation going to be? How many staff hours are likely to be required for detailed planning and implementation, and for appropriate staff development activities entailed by it? And so on. Only by careful (if sometimes subjective and impressionistic) costing of this kind is it possible to reach an informed conclusion about the feasibility of the project and to identify those costs which can be either avoided or reduced by revision to the plan.

Another task group should be detailed to *monitor the change* once it has been initiated. Evaluation of existing structures is done not simply to determine the need for change or, retrospectively, to determine the relative success of a programme for change, but ought to be undertaken as an on-going dimension of the programme itself. Evaluation needs to be illuminative (Parlett and Hamilton, 1972) and formative. It needs to cast light on the processes and procedures of the innovation as much as on the outcomes, and needs to provide regular feed-back to the team so that its insights help shape and refine the developing programme. Such a task-group will need to focus, first, on what is happening – this may require sensitive observation, the keeping of a diary, discussion and interviews with team-members, and the careful presentation of results to the group as a whole – and, later, on the value of what is happening. This will require the group to produce some criteria for the relative success of what is being introduced; or, more accurately, failure criteria which will signal early that things are not going according to plan. These criteria must be produced according to the precise shape which supportive education is to take in your particular school, but in terms of the model advanced in Chapter 4 above, the following criteria would be examples:

1 Are teachers seeking advice from the supportive specialist for production of alternative materials?
2 Are teachers still passing on learning problems to the supportive department rather than seeking advice on dealing with problems themselves?
3 Is there more liaison between teachers with pastoral duties and teachers with academic duties?
4 Are children more accepting and understanding of a distinction between those who need support and those who don't?
5 Do supportive specialists spend more time helping in the context of normal lessons?

If the answers are no to 2, but yes to the others, this *might or might not* mean that the innovation is succeeding. But, if the answers are yes to 2 and no to all the others, then this must surely be an indication that progress is not satisfactory.

Yet another task group might be set up to *plan a programme of staff-development activities* which might be aimed at the extended professionalism of staff, i.e. activities designed to develop skills in pedagogy, counselling, leadership, etc. These activities might then be incorporated in a series of lunch-time or after-school workshops, or form the basis of a number of one-day staff-development conferences. Some suggestions for such activities are presented below.

Some techniques for INSET

Classroom observation exercises

Most teachers complain that although they would like to be able to give each individual child personal attention, and would thus get to know the needs of each, constraints of time and numbers make this impossible. In fact, it is more often the case that it is the teacher's perception of his/her role as teacher, rather than either time or numbers, which gets in the way of a clearer understanding of the problems and processes of the child's learning. A significant means for raising teacher awareness of individual need is to allow the teacher to observe and converse with children in the classroom setting, but relieved of the duty of teaching them. Of course, this requires the co-operation of staff involved and approval for an additional member of staff to be present in the lesson but, if a reciprocal arrangement is agreed, this is mutually beneficial.

Observations may focus on a particular child who has already been identified as having special needs, though this must be very carefully and discreetly done lest the child or the class become aware, with the resulting labelling and stigmatisation of the subject. A checklist of features to be investigated is a useful start, although observations need to be followed up by talking with the child concerned. A general classroom checklist, on which the observer could record comments, may include items such as:

Objective Check to see whether the child's interpretation of the lesson coincides with the teacher's stated objective.

Materials Were the aids appropriate? Could others have been employed?

Language Did the teacher make use of questioning, explaining, encouragement, etc?

Situation How were the pupils involved in the lesson: talking, role play, writing, group work, etc?

Lesson What was the structure of the lesson: teacher talk, pupil discussion, then pupil written work, etc? How much use was made of recall, reinforcing past lessons and skills, etc?

Resources What resources were provided per pupil? What resources did the 'target' pupil make use of? Did the whole class tackle the same questions or was there differentiation of pupil tasks?

Grouping How was the class grouped? Where was the 'target' child sitting (front or back; by him/herself, etc)? Did the 'target' child summon help in the lesson? By what means and from whom was help sought (teacher, neighbour, copying, etc)?

Blackboard Did the child appear to understand, read or make use of material presented in this way?

Target child Check for hearing or sight problems. If present, did the child use the appropriate aid? Was his/her seating arrangement appropriate? Is the child left/right-handed? What type of behaviour did the child present during the lesson (boredom, lack of interest, totally absorbed, distracted, disruptive, co-operative, submissive, conforming, etc)? What type of personal involvement did the teacher use with this individual child (friendly, threatening, told off, encouraged, interested in progress), and vice versa? What questions or sections of the work did the child enjoy/not enjoy and why? What did the child find easy/hard?

Teacher How long did the teacher talk? How long were the pupils allowed to talk, question or discuss the material? What teaching style was used (dictation, copying notes, free/creative work, questions from a textbook or blackboard, lecture approach, investigation, etc)? What type of questions did the teacher ask? How did the teacher feel the lesson had gone for the 'target' child? Were there any lessons learned from this experience?

Marking Did the child make use of teacher's comments written in his or her exercise book? Were the comments helpful? Did the teacher go over the work with the individual?

A more demanding and itemised checklist, in which the 'target' child's behaviour is monitored at set intervals (say, every 30 seconds), might follow the pattern shown in Figure 10.

Obviously, each school could design a proforma to meet its individual needs. The sheet need not necessarily be used in the way described above. Instead, it might simply serve to raise the observer's awareness of actions occurring in the lesson and, bearing in mind the special needs of the child, offer the opportunity to witness a lesson from the child's perspective. Recent research in mathematics, for example, shows that idiosyncratic approaches to problem-solving may often account for poor performance, even though the strategies adopted by the child indicate considerable wisdom.

As we pointed out in Chapter 5, it is only by asking the child that we can ultimately establish *how* that child is or is not learning, and *how* that child is feeling and perceiving his/her situation. Subsequent discussion by the class teacher and the observer can raise the awareness of both, leading to a healthy self-examination by the teacher, and to suggestions for alternative approaches.

Micro-teaching

If a school has video-facilities, it is possible to set up a micro-teaching situation which allows the individual teacher and/or groups of teachers to observe and analyse their teaching performance. Counselling sessions and staff meetings can also be analysed in this way. In each case the agreement of all parties concerned is a prerequisite, and it has to be acknowledged that the presence of a video camera can be threatening indeed. However, if handled carefully, the results are worth the effort, allowing careful reflection on the all-important minutiae of verbal and non-verbal interaction: tone of voice, facial expression,

Figure 10

Date ....   Tutor Group ....

Lesson ....   Period ....

ON – TASK CHECKLIST

* = **Loss of concentration**

SEN child _____

Nature of lesson _____

Monitoring 'on-task' behaviour for a specified pupil every 30 seconds.

Time Lesson Starts		
Reading	1 story 2 pamphlet 3 research	
Listening	1 teacher 2 tape/video, etc 3 Others' views	
Watching		
Talking		
Writing	1 copying 2 creative 3 comprehension 4 computation	
Drawing		
Taping	1 resource 2 reply	
Misbehaving		
Asking Ques.	1 asking 2 answering	
Teacher/Child	direct involvement	
Phys. Activity	1 skill 2 exploratory 3 communication	
Praised		
Waits	1 hand raised 2 equipment 3 attention	
Other Activity		

listening skills and so on can be scrutinised in this way and the teacher's awareness of the *unspoken* message raised.

Some guidance and counselling is necessary for every supportive teacher – and that should mean every teacher – although some will need counselling skills to a greater degree than others. Real or simulated guidance or counselling sessions can be analysed to highlight problems of individual style, body language, unduly directive questioning, gestures of impatience, leading questions and so on. Ethical and moral questions can also be raised. Is it right to suggest to the child what his/her problem is, rather than to accept the child's own perception? Is it professionally unsound to lead a child to discuss problems emanating from the personal lives of others (e.g. his or her family) or from the behaviour of another staff member?

The uses to be made of the micro-teaching technique are so numerous that we cannot hope to cover its potential scope in the space of this section. We would, however, recommend that those who are interested in this approach review the wealth of literature available on this subject (Allen and Ryan, 1969; Borg, 1975; Brown, 1975).

Personal construct exercises

We are often unaware of the labelling that we engage in, especially where others are being identified as somehow abnormal or different. This is true of teachers as much as of anyone else and, although they may be vociferous in denying their practice, it is often clear to the observer that particular prejudices are at work. More fundamentally, teachers perceive children according to a variety of characteristics which are underpinned by such concepts as those of ability and energy. This perception of individual children is to *construe* them personally in a particular way, which often results in simplistic categorisation and stigmatising labels, e.g. this child is 'thick and lazy', that one 'bright and energetic'. How can we become more aware of what we do when we perceive the children we set out to teach or to help? Steve Decker, senior lecturer at Essex Institute of Higher Education, recommends the following group exercise aimed to do just that.

Collect some photographs of children *not* in your school – pop magazines or colour supplements will provide a good variety to work with – and give one to each teacher taking part. Ask each to write a brief description of his/her child in terms of personality, education and character, taking care that others do not see the photographs.

Shuffle the descriptions and stick them on the wall along with (but not matched with) the photographs. The group then guesses which description fits which photo. Ask the group to focus on the *categories* used in the descriptions. In this way the assumptions they are making about the nature of ability, the distribution of intelligence, gender, race and social class backgrounds, and how these relate to different kinds of problems or needs can be identified and explored. As always, care and sensitivity is needed: nothing is more painful than becoming aware of just how prejudiced one is.

Role play

We should always keep at the front of our minds the fact that the pupils we teach are a captive audience, who, in the majority of cases, are unable or reluctant to pass judgement on the relative merits of the education they receive. Instances of a child's commenting to the teacher on the degree to which the lesson has answered his or her needs are few and far between. The majority of pupils rarely question or refuse what is on offer, either by misbehaviour or truancy, as both offences tend to result in the individual's being punished rather than leading to an objective analysis of the situation which gave rise to such behaviours.

However, when teachers are put in the situation of being taught a lesson by a colleague, they are far less inhibited and much more likely to pin-point and verbalise any areas of difficulty or confusion, especially if we allocate them particular roles to perform during the lesson. The unfortunate teacher is aware that his or her 'friends' have been given identities and characteristics to display during the lesson, but is unaware exactly what they are. Following on from the lesson each 'pupil' reveals his or her special needs, which allows both the individual and the group to express an opinion on the degree to which they feel the lesson satisfied that particular need. The teacher can explain how he/she saw the problem and what steps were being taken to overcome it. It is hoped that the discussion will lead to a review of alternative strategies, approaches and methods that might have been employed to help the child and the different procedures the teacher could have taken to identify the need. We would hope that all concerned in these encounter groups would take the situation seriously but in a relaxed way, since it is necessary to avoid the possibility of some members taking offence.

Once again, this is a technique which is potentially threatening to members and carries with it considerable risks, as the experience of an in-service B.Ed. group testifies. In a unit dealing with teaching and learning, students – all experienced and qualified teachers – taught a typical lesson to their peers from other sectors: infant taught junior, junior taught secondary, secondary taught FE and so on. The group members were free to choose whatever pupil role they liked. Most went for the 'naughty child' role and as a result one student went home before it was her turn to teach, another was physically ill before teaching, and yet another reduced to tears. Obviously, an informative experience for all, but not one to be repeated.

Socio-drama

Rather than having everyone acting out a specific role in a particular situation, it is worth asking each participant to *empathise* with a role and then feed in how they imagine such a person would feel, and what responses might be expected from them. Each input adds to the colour and complexity of the developing picture, to which further responses are required. To start the ball rolling – and to ensure that the scenario is both realistic and useful – ask one member to be him/herself and to talk about a real problem he/she is facing.

An example might be a head of house who is genuinely unclear about what to do about a 'gifted' child who has stopped trying in the face of ridicule by other children. He/she talks through the dilemma and proposes a tentative course of action: to move the child to another class. Group members then empathise with as many significant others as practical, including the child; other children in his/her present class; children in the class to which he/she is to be moved; the teacher of the other class; the parents of the child; and so on. As each member feeds back his/her feelings in response to the proposal, the head of house reflects upon and revises his/her plan of attack. Not only does he/she benefit, but all members become more sensitive to the interests, feelings and perspectives of the range of people implicated in any such supportive decision.

'And then what do you think happened . . .?'

In this variant of the above, a series of events is written on pieces of paper and presented one by one to the group for discussion. After each input, the group is asked to consider the situation in terms of a number of key questions.

- Is this event to be welcomed or regretted?
- What are the positive and negative effects of this event likely to be?
- How should the school/the teacher react to this event?
- What would be the positive and negative effects of the proposed action?

Following a reasonable period for discussion a new input is made. An example of a sequence of events would be as follows:

> *Event 1* You are a member of the supportive education department. On Monday a child comes to you complaining that she cannot understand her maths teacher because he speaks so softly.
> *Event 2* On Tuesday, the head of maths moves this child from the top set to the middle set on the grounds that she is not achieving a sufficiently high standard in the subject.
> *Event 3* On Wednesday, the girl's mother writes to the school to complain that her child is being discriminated against because she is of West Indian origin.
> *Event 4* On Thursday, the girl's form tutor unearths a note from the primary school, in which the child is described as subject to occasional ear infections which may impair her hearing.
> *Event 5* On Friday, the child's head of year excludes her from a lunchtime club as a punishment for misbehaviour in her (new) maths class.

Job descriptions

One way of highlighting teachers' perceptions of both the nature of children's needs and the responsibility of specific teachers to provide appropriate support, is to ask the group to compose job specifications for particular roles in the school. This can be particularly enlightening – though potentially threatening – if the normal order of things is reversed and staff members are asked to devise 'job-specs' for their superiors, e.g. form tutors for pastoral middle managers, subject teachers for heads of faculty or department, middle managers for senior management, and so on. In the context of fostering supportive education, each task should focus on questions of authority, duties and accountability in respect of provision for children who are perceived as having particular needs or problems. Completed job descriptions can be used to explore concepts of need and the effectiveness of the school's existing supportive organisation.

Summary

It is our view that innovation in education generally is all too often undertaken with inadequate thought, planning or consideration of practical strategies for implementation. In this chapter we have argued that any attempt to move a school along the path from traditional styles of remedial and pastoral care towards the whole-school approach which we have styled supportive education is too significant to be allowed to founder through inadequate preparation. The gains are high but so, too, are the risks involved. The innovator must therefore consider carefully:

1 the nature of the proposed change in terms of such things as the scale of the innovation, the rate of change, resource implications, and effects on other parts of the school's provision;
2 a strategy for the management of innovation, to include an appraisal of staff attitudes to change and a plan for winning active support for the proposal;
3 the need for a programme of staff development and school-focused INSET implied by the new demands being made for enhanced professionalism both in the management/planning/administration sphere and in terms of practical skills in pedagogy, guidance, etc.

We have suggested some ways in which these issues might be approached, including the involvement of as many staff (and their disparate views) as possible in the early stages, with the subsequent delegation to task-groups of the detailed exploration and planning of change. Finally we have outlined a sample of specific staff-development exercises which schools might find useful in any attempt to heighten teachers' awareness of the problems of academic and pastoral support. These kinds of exercises are of value, whether linked to a specific proposed innovation or simply in the context of a school's on-going staff-development programme.

8 The network of support

Introduction

It would be presumptuous of any single profession to believe that it has the monopoly on the capacity to meet the needs of a particular child. Schools are but one part of a welfare network that has developed within our society to provide help and guidance and meet the diverse needs individuals may have at any stage in their life, a network which is by no means limited to the formal institutions which we associate with the welfare state. The extended family, the church and the various charitable and voluntary organisations have traditionally been parts of this framework of care and support. It must therefore be acknowledged from the start that the school is only one piece of a jig-saw puzzle in an extended network of agencies interested in catering for children's needs. Many of these agencies would claim to have a role to play in satisfying both academic and pastoral needs and may, quite rightly, be offended if their contribution is undervalued in the process of educating the child. Education must be seen in its more global setting if we are to overcome the myth that it is synonymous with schooling. For their part, teachers in schools must now readily accept education and teaching as being more than merely pouring the academic curriculum into an empty vessel.

None the less, many schools tend to be over-zealous in the way they guard their enclave, to the point where even parents are regarded as superfluous, to be treated with caution and involved only as a last resort. We would hope that the more obvious signs of this segregation – the notice at the gate beyond which parents are not allowed – are a thing of the past, and that schools are coming to see themselves as integral parts of a welfare network in which the sentiment (all too common in some staff rooms) that 'We're teachers, not social workers' is no longer acceptable. However, it is our view that the opportunities for genuine working partnerships with parents, welfare services and other agencies of all kinds have only just begun to be explored. For those seeking to provide a truly *supportive* education, this exploration must be a priority.

Working with parents

Despite a long series of prestigious and official reports (Newsom, 1963; Plowden, 1966; Court, 1976) the majority of schools underestimate, undervalue and underuse the contributions parents make in the education of their children. As an educational resource, the parents must be the most neglected items of teacher support, and the influence they have on their children is either barely grasped or else crudely cited as a factor in explaining poor performance. Yet even in this modern age the family remains the fundamental unit of organisation for personal and social life, and the role of the parent the single most important role in the welfare and socialisation of the next generation. That parents *should* have a crucial role in the formal education of their children seems obvious, yet the precise nature of the relationship between home and school is often unexplored.

In a review of the situation in the European Community, Macbeth (1985) points out that it is the parents who have the duty, in law, to educate the individual child, and argues that the responsibilities of the parents 'do not end at the school gates since parents do not divest themselves of their duty on passing a child to school; authority may be delegated but not responsibility . . . the education authority . . . must, by law, *make facilities available* to ensure that parents can carry out their educational duty' (pp117–8). He goes on to suggest that this has considerable implications not only for the obligations of parents, but also for their right, as clients, to expect accountability from those to whom they delegate authority. This, in turn, has serious consequences for the way teachers 'often nurse the argument that since they are professionals they are answerable to their consciences and to their peers', whereas, 'the prime accountability of pastoral care staff (and all teachers) is to parents until the young person is 16 years old'.

Accountability is only one part of the relationship, and not educationally the most significant. The relationships which exist and the interaction which takes place between parents and schools through correspondence, by telephone or face to face, is where concerted efforts to support and meet the needs of children are made or lost. In an interesting analysis, Roger Harris (1980, p167) draws our attention to a range of types of interaction which originate either with the school or with the parents, and which he summarises in Figure 11

Of these, he says '*parent-initiated* contacts can be classified according to the degree of involvement in school life which they generate', (p166) whereas the *school-initiated* contacts are categorised according to who or what provides the focus of attention. This is a curious classification since the former are ordered according to quality and process ('inquiring', 'supporting' and 'explaining') while the latter are not. Does this mean that the quality of process is taken for granted on the school's side while the value of parents' contributions is always problematic? Certainly, Harris's article tends to cast the school in the proactive role with the parental contribution seen as essentially reactive, and this imposes certain obligations on the schools: for example, the obligations to communicate clearly to parents, to help parents 'feel at ease and . . . to realise that their view is respected' and 'to adopt a welcoming attitude' (p168), aims which are not always realised on the ground. As Hanko (1985) summarises, 'teachers (need) to become more aware of the obstacles which might interfere from either side and to apply their insights to overcoming these through quite specific skills' (p105). This cannot, however, be achieved by individuals working in isolation.

The need for a school programme

All too often teachers leave parents' evenings complaining that the parents they really wished to see did not attend, but it is rare for teachers to do anything to resolve the situation or properly to investigate the reasons for the parents' absence. More often than not, it is interpreted simply as parental apathy or lack of interest in the education of their children and invoked to exonerate the teacher's and school's performance when children fail.

The fact that at many parent evenings it is the 'successful' child's parents who attend is revealing in itself. It would be interesting to discover whether these parents were also 'successful' and 'conforming' pupils at school. In Chapter 3 we made reference to the concept of fear, induced both accidentally and intentionally by teachers and schools in the policies and practices they adopt. It was Rogers (1967) who first drew our attention to the conditions of 'psychological safety' and 'psychological freedom' that children need in order to reveal their characters to the teacher and to the class. The same may be true for parents. Children who 'failed' in the education system become parents whose lasting impression of school is unlikely to be a favourable one.

Figure 11   *Types of parent-school interaction*

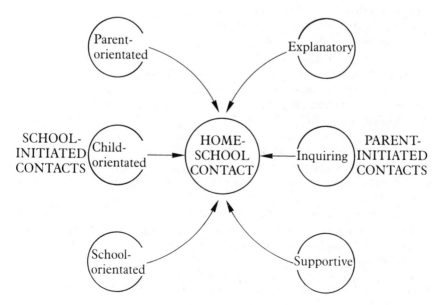

If the school was an alien place to them when they were children they have every reason to assume that little will have changed and that little can be achieved by initiating contact. Moreover, some parents still have a residual fear of certain situations they encountered in school, with the thought of having to confront the authority figure of the teacher once again a threat they cannot face.

To be concerned about a child with a special need – whether academic or pastoral – may only add to this fear. Afraid to hear the worst about their son or daughter, and fearing the stigma which would follow the classification of the child as a slow learner or maladjusted, such parents may well be forgiven their reluctance to respond to school initiatives or to take the initiative themselves. So schools will need to work especially hard with some parents if good and productive communication is to be achieved. However, we suggest that since support for *all* children is the aim, this extra effort needs to be grounded in a total environment which fosters good relations and positive parental involvement for *all* parents.

Marland (1985) has suggested that 'if schools are to work successfully with parents for the interlocked aims of the learning and welfare of the children, the individual action by a teacher is much more likely to be successful if there is an overall school programme' (pp100–102). Such a programme would include 'nineteen specific acts, activities, or policies which appear to be essential as a matrix of school/family links'. These are summarised below.

'Components of a programme

1   Good, informative printed brochures.
2   Opportunities to visit and question the school in advance of school-placement decision.
3   Full induction and reception interviews for both parents or guardians (if there are two).
4   A clear and accurate procedure for noting and promulgating the correct spelling, form, and pronunciation of both the family's and the pupil's names.
5   Efficient and pleasant reception and waiting arrangements for visitors.
6   Reliable message-taking arrangements.
7   A regular and carefully used Diary system.
8   Specific letters home on special matters, including praise.
9   Home visiting, both routine and for special purposes.
10   Reports.
11   Demonstration lessons.
12   Parent consultation meetings – to discuss individual progress.
13   Invitations to all quasi-public school events.
14   Courses on education.
15   Special Parent/Teacher social and cultural events.

16 Opportunities to join ordinary classes, or specially formed classes.

17 Opportunities for parental help.

18 Formal representation on any 'governing body' or 'school council' and a formal place in the consultation and decision-making of the school.

19 A conscious decision to look at the School's way of doing things from a parent's point of view.'

(Marland, 1985, pp100–102)

Our experience suggests that numbers 13 and 15 are especially important in developing an ethos of co-operation and involvement. In the school described in earlier chapters, full use has been made of school productions and pop concerts as a way of encouraging large numbers of parents to attend the school on a less formal basis, and this is no doubt true of many other schools.

Unfortunately, such events are often infrequent and perceived as a show-piece, which rarely allows the opportunity for large numbers of children to take part. Moreover, it often seems that the same old faces appear on these occasions. At Rickstones School the participation in concerts and shows has become a regular occurrence, providing opportunities for pupils to express their latent creative/dramatic talents. It is now established practice for tutor groups to lead the house assemblies. Many follow the Grange Hill scenario and examine teacher-pupil conflicts, others present a moral dilemma or crisis in another way, many are extensions of the work the tutor group has explored in drama lessons, whilst still others provide a more light-hearted entertainment value. In the course of a year tutor groups perform at least one ten- to fifteen-minute assembly and some, as it were, 'get the bug' and extend their audience by providing sketches for the complete upper or lower school. These performances have enabled the school to invite individual tutor group's parents to a private evening performance to enjoy a selection of sketches the tutor group has produced. The evening may be supplemented with children reading stories or poems they have written, musical offerings, displays of design work, demonstrations of apparatus used by children in, for example, 'modern maths', and rounded off with a play that has been produced especially for this occasion. Light refreshments can be provided and, as the children entertain their parents in the privacy of their own form room, the whole affair can be kept informal. While help from the design, humanities and drama departments is invaluable, the evening must be centred on the form and its tutor with perhaps the head of house (or year) as the only other member of staff in attendance. Amongst the benefits of such events is the fact that the parents have the all too rare opportunity of hearing only praise for their children's efforts.

It is also important to emphasise the positive wherever possible in the more traditional parents' evenings. Understandably, parents do not relish the idea of being lectured to or of hearing a catalogue of their child's misdemeanours.

If the point of the interview was merely to expect the parents to go away and discipline the child for unacceptable behaviours in school, it is reasonable for parents to resent this request and to expect the school to resolve such professional problems itself. It would not take long for attitudes to harden on both sides, with the parents seeing only 'teacher incompetence' whilst the teachers see only 'un co-operative parents'. Schools tend to take the concept of supportive or co-operative parents to mean that the parents take the school's side against the child, whereas the parents who are most supportive of their children are quite likely to defend them in such circumstances, pointing out that they are no bother at home and even (with some justice) pointing out the mis-management by some teachers! Inevitably, with such a confrontation the outcome of the meeting will be unlikely to benefit the child, and in place of a concerted initiative it can rapidly degenerate into one of conflict.

Where parents are involved from the start and the school is seen genuinely as being on the child's side and sincerely wishing to help, parents and teachers find themselves in a more relaxed atmosphere where it is easier to reflect on the other's point of view. Under these conditions there is every reason to expect the growth of a working partnership between parents and teachers, whose shared concern is the best interests of the child. After all, in the majority of cases, parents are the prime carers for their own children and few would wantonly destroy the opportunity to establish an effective teaching partnership with the school.

But parents *do* need to understand what the school is trying to do and may well be put off schemes which represent a break with their own experience. Parents whose own schooling was streamed from start to finish and whose children received special provision in remedial groups in the junior school, will find the organisation of supportive education, exemplified in Rickstones School, bewildering if it is not properly explained to them. In this respect, Marland's (1985) emphasis on information brochures and full induction and reception interviews is well placed, and opportunities for parents to *see* supportive education in progress would be valuable indeed.

Welfare roles

Interaction between home and school is often mediated or supplemented by the work of agencies with more or less specific responsibilities for the educational welfare of children. These agencies include the educational welfare officer, school medical officer, the child guidance clinic, probation officers, health visitors, social workers, the educational psychologist, careers officers, and specialist therapists in speech, hearing, and so on, while voluntary agencies like the NSPCC provide an exemplary supplementary service. This is an impressive array of roles and the potential for co-ordinated action is considerable, yet neither parents nor schools appear to take full advantage of what is on offer.

Many parents are anxious and wary of outside agencies, seeing them as a threat to be avoided at all costs. Professionals working for these agencies may be treated with suspicion as someone 'spying' on the family. With the increasing incidence of a break-down in the nuclear family, many parents are unsure of whom to turn to for help and advice. In the management of everyday crises parents often resort to seeking neighbourly advice from someone who has experienced or presently faces a similar predicament. Perhaps as a response to this and accelerated by the decline in extended family contact, the past decade has seen the emergence and growth of self-help groups, organised to assist individuals in coming to terms with certain problems. But, when it comes to special educational needs, the number of such groups is small, with (for whatever reason) the Dyslexia Association being the most prominent. The family doctor was once the focal point for much advice, but many parents now feel a reluctance to intrude on the doctor's time with matters they perceive as not directly medical issues, and it has to be said that the GP may simply lack the training and expertise necessary to give much guidance on social, emotional or educational problems. Social workers may have much to offer, but enlisting their support still carries a stigma and the matter can be out of control before parents resort to this option.

In such instances there is room for a half-way stage and the educational welfare officer (EWO) seems ideally placed to fill an important gap, providing a clear link between home and school. The days when this role was defined merely in terms of a truant officer have long since passed, with the *caring* side of the work now receiving more emphasis; yet for some parents the image of 'the school board man' is still a powerful one. Properly understood (and properly integrated into the work of the school), the EWO is a valuable link, meeting regularly with heads of house/year, senior pastoral staff and those involved with special (behavioural) needs, and with parents in their own homes.

The educational psychologist is another important resource for the school, although we have made it clear in earlier chapters that the identification of this role exclusively with simplistic notions of testing and assessment is unhelpful. In the wake of Warnock (1978), most authorities have increased the number of educational psychologists in their employ and usually deploy them in teams to service a particular part of the authority's area. What is needed is a realisation of the importance of *context* for the work of this member of the welfare team. Knowledge of the school and its environment is important, and regular consultation between schools and the psychological service is crucial if their help in clarifying problems, specific assessment, advice on specific techniques for considering behaviour and evaluating progress is to be utilised to the full. And, of course, the educational psychologist is in the key position of notifying the authority of those children who may have special educational needs requiring formal assessment under section 5 of the 1981 Education Act, (commonly referred to as a 'statement').

Unfortunately, as with most of the other parts of the network of welfare agencies, the work of the psychologist tends to take place behind closed doors. In secondary schools, in particular, there are all too few instances of the educational psychologist working alongside the teacher in the classroom and integrating a programme of support to complement the normal curriculum. All that many teachers know of the educational psychologist's presence in school is the withdrawal of a child from their lesson and a room set aside for the interview, usually with a notice, *Do not disturb* or *In conference* on the door! Feedback to teachers is usually second-hand and is often made worse when wrapped up in jargon. Unless time is allocated for feedback sessions to appropriate members of the teaching staff, the value of this service, as with all others, is severely curtailed.

The welfare network

Much could be said about each of the other agencies mentioned above, but it is not our purpose to describe all the individual roles which make up the network. (For descriptions of a variety of these roles, see Johnson (1980) and Murgatroyd (1980)). What is more appropriate here is to note some features of the network as a whole. Welton (1982) has grouped these under three headings:

'a School Based   e.g. teachers, school-based social
                          workers, school counsellors,
 b School Attached   e.g. the educational psychologist,
                          educational welfare officer,
                          school nurse, and
 c Community Based   e.g. social workers, police juvenile
                          liaison officers, probation officers
                          and general practitioners.'

Whilst there may be a reasonable degree of co-operation between the school-based and school-attached agencies, the relationships between these two and community-based agencies is more tenuous. A reason for this may lie in the traditional concept each agency holds of the service it provides. In all of the agencies mentioned above there are individual members of professions who are reluctant to move from a narrowly defined or restricted role conception, placing their emphasis on the traditional core concept of the job.

However, others take a broader or more extended view of their role and recognise the 'need to integrate their work with that of others within their own or another profession working with the same child or family' (Welton, 1985, p64). Welton's recent work suggests that the latter is perhaps becoming the more common view:

> 'The two most striking findings . . . are, firstly, the very broad
> professional orientation of the professions sampled, and, secondly,
> the very few cases where respondents claim that a child's needs
> can be met entirely within their own profession or agency. With

certain exceptions it may be concluded that each profession sampled had a broad rather than restricted view of its responsibility for children's needs, and that in general the respondents recognised the necessity of working in some way with members of other professions either in co-operation or by referring children to them.' (p68)

Unfortunately, the historical development and emergent sub-cultures of each welfare profession, and thus the tradition within which individual practitioners are trained, varies significantly. Successful co-operation requires a measure of mutual respect, trust and understanding which, in many instances, simply does not exist.

'Rather than knowledge and understanding, the welfare network is riddled with myths and ignorance about the work of other professions, some of which are based on occupational stereotypes, others on ignorance of developments in a particular profession. Common myths include the beliefs that most educational welfare officers are ex-policeman with two left feet; teachers cannot be trusted with confidential information; social workers are young, inexperienced and idealistic do-gooders who are here today and gone tomorrow; medical doctors refuse to share information, and psychologists are usually in need of their own attention.' (p77)

In another piece of research, Daphne Johnson (Johnson *et al* 1980) comments that 'although teachers claimed to have little knowledge of or contact with agency practitioners, generalisations were readily offered about, for example, the youth, personal style and impermanence of social workers, or the medical profession's obsession with confidentiality'.

Against this background of ignorance and prejudice, it is hardly surprising that co-operation is often lacking, not least over issues of confidentiality and professional jurisdiction. Nor should it be surprising that in a recent study of pastoral care and welfare networks (Johnson, 1985) Johnson found a general picture emerging 'of many practitioners working hard on behalf of often overlapping groups of clients, but with little awareness or understanding of the efforts being made in adjacent services'.

Johnson went on to identify a number of factors which further complicate school/agency co-operation. These include:

' ● differences in geographical areas over which they have jurisdiction: primary and secondary school catchment areas do not necessarily tie in with each other, nor with school health areas or the 'patch' of the same social-work team;
  ● differences in the age-ranges of clients: for example, the police juvenile bureau is concerned only for the 10 to 17 year age range whereas social workers cater for clients 'from cradle to grave';

- differences in pattern and conditions of work: where hours worked are different, with the presence or absence of flexi-time, and where different holiday entitlement and so on apply, the practical arrangements for 'working together' cannot be taken for granted;
- differences in status and seniority: exemplified by the low pay and poor professional status of the EWO when compared with teachers and other agency professionals;
- differences in modes of work: e.g. collaborative work centred on the out-of-school case-conference is 'normal' for the social worker but practically impossible (and certainly 'foreign') to most teachers.'

(Johnson, 1985, pp102–106)

For both teachers and agencies, problems of weaving their work in with that of others are clearly considerable, and the implications of this for the child are frightening. Murgatroyd's (1980) collection of case-studies in *Helping the Troubled Child* is dominated by the difficulties of timing and co-ordinating interventions by helpers from different agencies, breakdowns in communication, poor liaison and inter-professional distrust and suspicion. Some of these cases are presented from the perspective of the teacher and tend to convey a picture of the teacher whose best efforts are frustrated by the inefficiency of the outside agencies. In the case of Karen, for example, (Gregson, 1980) the situation was characterised by 'a tangle of conflicting purposes, unstated private intentions, and unco-ordinated actions, which was to stifle and frustrate those involved . . . over the next two years', (pp109–102), a situation attributable not least to delay and cancelled appointments on the part of the child guidance clinic.

Yet schools must accept their share of the blame, too. We cannot include in our vocation a commitment to pastoral and academic support, which includes making recommendations on individual special educational needs, strengthening home-school links, and collaboration with welfare services and other agencies (Johnson, 1985, p100), if we do not first put our own house in order. And this 'house' has psychological, inter-professional and structural dimensions to it. As Hanko (1985) has pointed out, teachers can be apprehensive about working together with other professions, but teachers are the first to refute the view that this is an insurmountable problem, once appropriate support groups have been established. It is true that teachers must, first, be willing to re-think their attitudes and unpack their prejudices about the profession whose collaboration they require. Second, they must be positive and welcoming in their inter-personal encounters with these agents – after all, it is not only *parents* who find the school a forbidding institution: many a social worker and educational psychologist has been put off by the anonymity of the large school and by the luke-warm reception they receive on their visits. And, third, schools must devise proper systems and structures of roles into which such agencies can be properly 'plugged'. As Craft (1980) summed up: '*co-ordination, team* functioning, and a *clear channel* for referral are felt to be basic concepts. The more rational and co-ordinated pattern of neighbourhood social services . . . will help little, if schools do nothing to rationalise *their* internal resources.'

It is our view that a shared philosophy of supportive education and the clear system of roles and procedures which this would entail, are the foundations of such a rationalisation.

Conclusion

Because of their rhetorical force, it is all too easy to use words like 'team' and 'liaison' to dignify what is in fact a haphazard sequence of unco-ordinated encounters, characterised by lack of shared objectives and procedures and bedevilled by boundary disputes and poor communication. In this respect, it is not only teachers who need the kind of staff development advocated in the last chapter, but also members of the various welfare and related professions discussed above. Both in- and out-school agents require a raised awareness of the nature of other welfare roles, and in this, both formal and informal contacts are important. However, as Welton (1985) points out, neither will achieve much if there are not 'appropriate formal systems of welfare co-ordination at policy-making, administrative and professional levels' (p75).

Such a plea is for reform at levels higher than that of the school, yet this does not mean that individual schools and their teachers are impotent. We believe much can be done through regular meetings between pastoral, special needs or supportive staff and their local EWOs, psychologists and the like, and through exercises in awareness-raising and staff development which focus on a multi-professional approach to meeting children's needs. We submit that it is within the power of the staff of any school to initiate action leading to this end, and such action is a natural accompaniment to the model of supportive education which this book has advanced.

9 Getting it together

Despite the force of recent critiques of schooling – many of which we have utilised in this book – our state system of education has a human face. This is the face of the teacher who is sympathetic to the child facing an impediment to learning, the teacher who is concerned that a child is unhappy and insecure or preoccupied with problems too personal to share, the teacher who sacrifices his/her family life to counsel parents and attend parents' evenings, the EWO who works all the hours God sends to protect the child at risk, and the social worker who loses sleep worrying about whether or not an intervention is necessary. All these and others, too, are committed to the care and welfare of the individual child, and we must not allow the current demoralisation of the caring professions to distract attention from the great good which they do.

However, they labour in an environment of physical resources and organisational structures which may provide little help and many obstructions to their endeavour. They function in an intellectual and cultural environment characterised by ambiguity, and lack of clarity and shared understandings. In short, we have many carers from diverse traditions, employing concepts which are dubious, within structures that are unhelpful, based on assumptions that are archaic. Care in education needs enlightenment, rationalisation, co-ordination and a unification of purpose.

A particularly vivid division is to be found in every comprehensive school in which different people are identified as responsible for pastoral care and special educational needs. As the tale of Jimmy Stephens, with which this book begins, illustrates, this is an artificial distinction which over-simplifies the complexity of children's needs and can set carer against carer. This book has been an attempt to acknowledge the complexities and problems of the academic, pastoral and special needs dimensions of schools.

We believe that certain concepts dominate our thinking and determine our perceptions of the problem. These concepts include the idea that there is something called the 'normal' to which most children belong and that only those who are not normal require particular care; the idea that there is one 'ability' which is distributed in a particular pattern throughout the population; and the concept of 'failure', applying to those who do not conform to the expectations of a prevailing sub-culture. Taken together, these concepts and the assumptions which they make constitute that most powerful of myths from which so much of our schooling derives its shape.

In the formal organisation of our schools this myth is given substance in both the structures of roles and grouping practices and the daily procedures in which teachers engage. Through streaming, setting, banding and the creation of sink groups of remedial children and special units for disruptives, we institutionalise the segregation of the abnormal from the normal, confirm the prevailing notions of differences in intellectual ability, and perpetuate the tendency to attribute failure to the cultural, moral and inter-personal deficiencies of the child, the family and the neighbourhood. Our daily practices within this environment continually reduce learning to an unfair competition, submit to and sometimes applaud the tyranny of testing, and generally defend and conserve a curriculum ill-suited to many of the needs with which *all* children present us. Traditional structures influence the views schools have of their clientele, the views teachers have of their charges, the views pupils have of their peers and the view the child has of himself. We encourage conformity to the status quo, all too often promoting a narrow and closed approach to learning which results in a dependency quite inimical to the central values embodied in the concept of education.

For most children and for most teachers, the school seems to do all this in a social and professional vacuum. The range of professional agencies and related cultural institutions which comprise an extended welfare network are rarely acknowledged to exist, let alone embraced as colleagues in a common pursuit. The different traditions, perspectives and routines fragment the work of the home, the church, the social services and so on, while teachers with specific responsibility for pastoral care and special needs remain largely ignorant of their roles and functions.

Our critique has inevitably involved some fundamental criticism of the mainstream curriculum which schools offer, for in the last analysis it is here that such categories as 'failure', the 'normal' and the 'problem child' are identified. Children who conform to expectations conceived in a model of product teaching in which the three Rs are still pivotal are apparently not problems and do not appear to have needs either! Those who fail in the quality control of assessment within this narrow definition of ability are undervalued and their manifold talents ignored. Throughout this whole process, the invidious labelling, segregation and special attention they receive generate a powerful self-fulfilling prophecy which may be finally recognised as a means of social control which is profoundly conservative in distracting attention from the inadequacies of schooling.

In this book we have attempted to challenge both the conventional wisdom and the conventional practices which are usually associated with remedial education and pastoral care. To counter the lack of clarity in different conceptions of care we have proposed that schools see their response to individual needs as having two related emphases. Children do need support, and although their needs are not always easily classified, we suggest that some responses focus on difficulties in learning and understanding (which we have called *learning support*) while others focus on problems of personal, inter-personal and emotional adjustment (which we have termed *pastoral support*).

We reject the idea that schools need to concentrate on 'special' children since it is our view that *every* child has needs, and that these needs include support in learning, in self-analysis and in moral support as persons rather than pupils. We have therefore argued that such divisive and emotive labels as 'remedial child' and 'pastoral problem' should give way to a broad concept of supportive education.

This entails an attack on the present division and isolationism of different agencies in the welfare network at large and of the remedial, academic and pastoral camps inside our schools. We have argued that learning support and pastoral support need to be integrated within the school and have offered an example of how one school has attempted to achieve this. We have further argued that a co-ordination of the work of such welfare agents as the educational psychologist, the EWO, and the child guidance clinic is long overdue, and needs to be undertaken in collaboration with supportive staff involved in pastoral and special needs provision in schools. The case conference in which a number of individuals talk at cross purposes in an attempt to solve a problem which they do not even define in the same way, and in the absence of appropriate school staff, is surely unacceptable.

The kinds of change we are advocating require fundamental changes in schools' perceptions of their role. While schools accept the responsibility for actively providing the set of learning experiences comprising the curriculum, they have traditionally seen their role in both remedial education and pastoral care as *reactive*. What we are proposing is that, through a substantial reform of the curriculum (including the planning of a pastoral curriculum) and the integration of supportive specialists in the mainstream of teaching in 'normal' lessons, schools become *proactive* in identifying, anticipating, and providing for a wide range of individual needs. To do this, schools must recognise that true education is non-competitive and concerned with the development of each individual to the fullest extent possible.

It is for this reason that we have rejected a product model of teaching in favour of the recognition that education is a developmental and enriching process. The plain fact is that the traditional academic curriculum is closed to many children because it requires specific skills of literacy for access. Our society has mistaken the product of a literate and numerate populace for the process of individual enrichment. Not only are children refused such enrichment on the grounds that they simply can't read: they have also been undervalued as a social resource. To ignore the talents and to deny the development of those talents is not simply a loss for the individual but a loss to society as a whole. The perspective of supportive education requires us to value equally the valid contribution of every child. This is only possible if we are willing to accept the possibility that many children need learning support and pastoral support precisely because the curriculum we offer is either inappropriate or closed to them. We have argued that the curriculum can be made much more open through an enlightened approach to pedagogy. This does not necessarily require a full-blown programme of resource-based learning. We suggest that new technologies of quite humble proportions (and we have used the example of the personal cassette recorder) have barely begun to be recognised in most schools. As for the potential for individualised learning of information technology generally, most schools have not even begun to explore them seriously.

It is sad but true that schools have suitable hardware and software sitting in cardboard boxes while remedial teachers are still teaching the three Rs by chalk and talk method and complaining about the size of their classes!

To achieve change is far from easy. For one thing, it will involve a change in both assumptions and practices which are ingrained in the teaching profession. Against the norm-related testing and classification of whole groups of children, teachers, first, must accept the need to relate assessment to the understanding of the individual child's experience from that child's point of view. Second, against the segregation by ability of children with special needs teachers need to accept that every class contains a mixture of abilities, tastes, interests and talents, and that supportive education requires the integration of diversity. Against the tendency to encourage conformity, dependence and closed thinking, supportive education must strive to foster independence of work and thought.

These prescriptions require a raising of teachers' awareness, which in many cases can only be described as revolutionary. Not only must the long-standing assumptions about the nature of intelligence, ability, and normal behaviour be challenged: the organisational structures of schools need to be seriously questioned. Integrating a handful of enlightened carers is likely to achieve little if the school continues to embody division and segregation through such practices as streaming and withdrawal – and, in extreme cases, transfer to special institutions – and through the perpetuation of the pastoral/academic split. There will be those, of course, who will reject any criticism of existing arrangements on the grounds of vested interest, seeing integration as a threat to their personal empires and in some cases to their jobs.

Such anxiety is understandable and in one sense justified since some specialist roles as we know them would cease to exist. However, if every teacher is to be seen as a supportive teacher, then the need for specialists who can lead, co-ordinate and train teachers for this aspect of their work, and whose particular expertise will be an essential supplement to the daily work of the classroom, will be greater rather than less. While it may be comfortable for specialists to remain aloof from the hurly-burly of ordinary classroom teaching, this is not an indulgence to be afforded at the expense of the child. For it is, after all, in the daily experience of the ordinary lesson that problems appear and need to be tackled. To accept the prevailing system is to condone a set of structures and practices which reflect the needs of a conservative society and protect the interests of teachers rather than those of the children for whom schools supposedly exist.

We do not pretend for a moment that this book has provided solutions to that multiplicity of problems of which the remedial department and the pastoral care structure are symptoms. However, we do believe that the developments that have characterised special needs education and pastoral care in recent years have created a state of flux in which an initiative like supportive education could well be favourably received. This book is offered as a basis for discussion in schools which are genuinely committed to evaluating and improving the support they give to each and every child.

References

Ablewhite, R. 1977: 'What is Remedial Education?' In Widlake P. (ed): *Remedial Education: Programmes and Progress*. London: Longmans.

Allen, D. and Ryan, K. 1969: *Microteaching*. Reading, Mass: Addison-Wesley.

Aron, R. 1968: *Main Currents in Sociological Thought* Vol 2. Harmondsworth: Penguin.

Baldwin, J. and Wells, H. 1979: *Active Tutorial Work* (1–5). Oxford: Blackwell.

Balow, B. 1971: 'Perceptual-motor activities in the treatment of severe reading disability' In *Reading Teacher* Vol 24.

Barnes, D., Britten, J. and Rosen, H. 1971: *Language, the Learner and the School*. Harmondsworth: Penguin.

Bernstein, B. 1971: 'On the Classification and Framing of Educational Knowledge' In Young, M.F.D. (ed), *Knowledge and Control*. London: Collier-MacMillan.

Bernstein, B. 1972: 'Social Class, Language and Socialisation'. In *Language in Education: A Source Book*. London: Routledge and Kegan Paul and The Open University Press.

Best, R. (in progress in 1986): 'A study of the Organisation of Remedial Provision in Two Comprehensive Schools' unpublished PhD dissertation. University of East Anglia.

Best, R. 1985: 'Concept of Welfare and Ability in Remedial Education'. In Ribbins, P. (ed), *Schooling and Welfare*. Lewes: Falmer.

Best, R., Jarvis, C. and Ribbins, P. 1977: 'Pastoral Care: Concept and Process'. *British Journal of Educational Studies* Vol XXV, No 2, June.

Best, R., Jarvis, C. and Ribbins, P. (eds) 1980: *Perspectives on Pastoral Care*. London: Heinemann.

Best, R. and Ribbins, P. 1983: 'Rethinking the Pastoral/Academic Split'. *Pastoral Care in Education* Vol 1, No 1.

Best, R., Ribbins, P., Jarvis, C. and Oddy, D. 1983: *Education and Care*. London: Heinemann.

Beswick, N. 1977: *Resource-based Learning*. London: Heinemann.

Black, H. 1982: 'The Prospects for Public Examinations in England and Wales', *Educational Analysis Vol 4, No 3*.

Black, H. and Dockrell, W. 1980: *Diagnostic Assessment in Secondary Schools*. Edinburgh: SCRE.

Blackburn, K. 1975: *The Tutor*. London: Heinemann.

Blackburn, K. 1983: *Head of House, Head of Year*. London: Heinemann.

Bloom, B. 1976: *Human Characteristics and School Learning*. New York: McGraw-Hill.

Borg, W. 1975: 'Moving Towards a Breakthrough in Teacher Education'. *Education USA* Vol 95.

Bowles, S. and Gintis, H. 1976: *Schooling in Capitalist America*. New York: Basic Books.

Brennan, W. 1971: 'A Policy for Remedial Education'. *Remedial Education* Vol 6, No 1.

Brennan, W. 1974: *Shaping the Education of Slow Learners*. London: Routledge and Kegan Paul.

Brennan, W. 1978: *Reading for Slow Learners*. London: Evans/Methuen.

Broadfoot, P. 1985: 'Profiles and Pastoral Care: Some Neglected Questions'. In Lang, P. and Marland, M. (eds), *New Directions in Pastoral Care*. Oxford: Blackwell.

Brown, G. 1975: *Microteaching*. London: Methuen.

Buckley, J. 1980: 'The Care of Learning: Some Implications for School Organisation'. In Best, R. et al (eds), *Perspectives on Pastoral Care*. London: Heinemann.

Burt, C. 1952: *The Causes and Treatment of Backwardness*. London: University of London Press.

Burt, C. 1937: *The Backward Child*. London: University of London Press.

Button, L. 1974: *Developmental Group Work with Adolescents*. London: Hodder and Stoughton.

Button, L. 1981–2: *Group Tutoring for the Form Teacher (1–2)*. London: Hodder and Stoughton.

Carnoy, M. 1974: *Education as Cultural Imperialism*. New York: McKay.

Chin, R. and Benne, K. 1974: 'General Strategies for Effecting Change in Human Systems'. In Bennis, K. et al, *The Planning of Change*. London: Holt, Rinehart and Winston.

Cippolla, C. 1969: *Literacy and Developments in the West*. Baltimore: Penguin Books.

Clark, M. 1979: 'Why Remedial? Implications of using the concept of Remedial Education'. In Gains, C. et al (eds), *Remedial Education: Guidelines for the Future*. London: Longman.

Clunies-Ross, L. and Wimhurst, S. 1983: *The Right Balance: Provision for Slow Learners in Secondary Schools*. Windsor: NFER-Nelson.

Coles, G. 1978: 'The Learning Disabilities Test Battery: Empirical and Social Views'. *Harvard Educational Review* Vol 48, No 3, August.

Corbishley, P. and Evans, J. 1980: 'Teachers and Pastoral Care: An Empirical Comment'. In Best, R. et al (eds), *Perspectives on Pastoral Care*. London: Heinemann.

Cowans, S. 1974: 'The Education of Slow Learning Pupils'. *Secondary Education* Vol 4, No 4, September.

Cowell, B. and Wilson, J. 1984: 'Pastoral Care: Some Prevailing Fantasies'. *Pastoral Care in Education* Vol 2, No 2, June.

..

Craft, M. 1980: 'School Welfare Roles and Networks'. In M. Craft et al (eds), *Linking Home and School*. London: Harper and Row.

Craft, M. and Lytton, H. (eds) 1969: *Guidance and Counselling in British Schools*. London: Edward Arnold.

Craft, M. Raynor, J. and Cohen, L. (eds) 1980: *Linking Home and School*. London: Harper and Row.

Davies, L. 1980: 'The Social Construction of Low Achievement'. In Raybould E. et al, *Helping the Low Achiever in the Secondary School*. Educational Review Occasional Publication No 7.

Department of Education and Science 1963: *Half Our Future*. London: HMSO. (The Newsom Report)

Department of Education and Science 1967: *Children and Their Primary Schools*. London: HMSO. (The Plowden Report)

Department of Education and Science 1971: *Slow Learners in Secondary Schools* Survey 15. London: HMSO.

Department of Education and Science 1975: *A Language For Life*. London: HMSO. (The Bullock Report)

Department of Education and Science 1978: *Special Educational Needs*. London: HMSO. (The Warnock Report)

Department of Education and Science 1984: *Records of Achievement: a statement of policy*. London: HMSO.

Department of Health and Social Security 1976: *Fit For The Future*. London: HMSO. (The Court Report)

Dooley, S. 1980 'The Relationship between the Concepts of "Pastoral Care" and "Authority"'. In Best, R. et al (eds), *Perspectives on Pastoral Care*. London: Heinemann.

Edwards, J. 1983: 'Remedial Education Post-Warnock: interment or revival?' *Remedial Education* Vol 18, No 1.

Epps, S., Ysseldyke, J. and McGue, M. 1984: '"I Know One When I See One" – Differentiating LD and Non-LD Students'. *Learning Disabilities Quarterly* Vol 7, Winter.

Edwards, R. and Gibbon, V. 1973: *Words Your Children Use*. London: Burke.

Farr, R. 1969: *Reading: What can be Measured?* Newark, Delaware: International Reading Association.

Gains, C. 1980: 'Remedial Education in the 1980s'. *Remedial Education* Vol 15, No 1.

Gains, C. and McNicholas, J. (eds)(1979): *Remedial Education: Guidelines for the Future*. London: Longman.

Gipps, C. and Goldstein, H. 1984: 'More than a Change in Name?' *Special Education* Vol 11, No 4.

Golby, M. and Gulliver, J. 1979: 'Whose Remedies, Whose Ills? A critical review of remedial education'. *Curriculum Studies* Vol 11, No 2.

Green, L. 1969: 'Comparison of School Attainment'. *Special Education* Vol 58, No 2.

Gregson, M. 1980: 'Karen: a difficult girl'. In Murgatroyd, S. (ed), *Helping the Troubled Child*. London: Harper and Row.

Gulliford, R. 1971: *Special Educational Needs*. London: Routledge and Kegan Paul.

Gurney, R. 1976: *Language, Learning and Remedial Teaching*. London: Edward Arnold.

Haigh, G. 1975: *Pastoral Care*. London: Pitman.

Haigh, G. 1977: *Teaching Slow Learners*. London: Temple Smith.

Hallahan, D. and Cruickshank, W. 1973: *Psycho-Educational Foundations of Learning Disabilities*. New Jersey: Prentice Hall.

Hallahan, D. and Kauffman, J. 1977: 'Labels, categories, behaviours:? ED, LD, EMR reconsidered'. *Journal of Special Education* Vol 11.

Halsell, E. 1973: *The Comprehensive School*. London: Pergamon.

Hamblin, D. 1978: *The Teacher and Pastoral Care*. Oxford: Blackwell.

Hamblin, D. 1981: *Teaching Study Skills*. Oxford: Blackwell.

Hamblin, D. 1983: *Guidance 16–19*. Oxford: Blackwell.

Hanko, G. 1985: *Special Needs in Ordinary Classrooms*. Oxford: Blackwell.

Hargreaves, A. 1985: 'Motivation versus Selection: A dilemma for records of personal achievement'. In Lang, P. and Marland, M. (eds) *New Directions in Pastoral Care*. Oxford: Blackwell.

Hargreaves, D. 1972: *Interpersonal Relations and Education*. London: Routledge and Kegan Paul.

Hargreaves, D. 1980: 'Social Class, the Curriculum, and the Low Achiever'. In Raybould, E. et al (eds), *Helping the Low Achiever in the Secondary School*. Educational Review Occasional Publications No 7.

Hargreaves, D. 1982: *The Challenge for the Comprehensive School*. London: Routledge and Kegan Paul.

Hargreaves, D. 1984: *Improving Secondary Schools*. London: ILEA. (The Hargreaves Report)

Harris, R. 1980: 'Parent-Teacher contacts – a case-study'. In Craft, M. et al (eds), *Linking Home and School*. London: Harper and Row.

Havering Policy Document 1983: *Providing for Special Educational Needs – A Guide to Schools*. London Borough of Havering: unpublished.

Hewitt, F. 1974: *Education of Exceptional Learners*. Boston: Allyn and Bacon.

Holmes, G. 1986: 'Change and Innovation in Pastoral Care', *Pastoral Care in Education*, forthcoming.

Holt, J. 1965: *How Children Fail*. London: Pitman.

Hughes, P. 1980: 'Pastoral Care - the Historical Context'. In Best, R. et al (eds), *Perspectives on Pastoral Care*. London: Heinemann.

Illich, I. 1973: *Deschooling Society*. Harmondsworth: Penguin.

Irving, A. 1982: *Starting to Teach Study Skills*. London: Edward Arnold.

James, C. 1968: *Young Lives at Stake*. London: Collins.

Johnson, D. 1985: 'Pastoral Care and the Welfare Network'. In Lang, P. and Marland, M. (eds), *New Directions in Pastoral Care*. Oxford: Blackwell.

Johnson, D. and Myklebust, H. 1967: *Learning Disabilities: Educational Principles and Practices*. New York: Grune and Stratton.

Johnson, D., Ransom, E., Packwood, T., Bowden, K., and Kogan, M. 1980: *Secondary Schools and the Welfare Network*. London: Allen and Unwin.

Kirk, S. 1975: 'Behavioural Diagnosis and Remediation of Learning Disabilities'. In Kirk, S. and McCarthy, J. (eds), *Learning Disabilities: Selected ACLD Papers*. Boston: Houghton Mifflin.

Kirk, S. and Elkins, J. 1975: 'Characteristics of Children Enrolled in the Child Service Demonstration Centres'. *Journal of Learning Disabilities* Vol 8.

Kirk, S. and McCarthy, J. (eds) 1975: *Learning Disabilities: Selected ACLD Papers*. Boston: Houghton Mifflin.

Lang, P. 1982: *Pastoral Care: Concern or Contradiction?* Unpublished MA thesis. University of Warwick.

Lang, P. 1983: 'Perspectives on Pastoral Care'. *Pastoral Care in Education* Vol 1, No 1.

Lang, P. and Marland, M. (eds) 1985: *New Directions in Pastoral Care*. Oxford: Blackwell.

Lawrence, P. and Lorsch, J. 1969: *Developing Organisations*. Reading, Mass: Addison-Wesley.

Leach, D. and Raybould, E. 1977: *Learning and Behaviour Difficulties in Schools*. London: Open Books.

Leighs, P. 1977: 'Great Expectations: A Consideration of the Self-fulfilling Prophecy in the Context of Educability'. *Educational Review* Vol 29.

Macbeth, A. 1985: 'Parents, Schools and Pastoral Care: Some Research Priorities'. In Lang, P. and Marland, M. (eds), *New Directions in Pastoral Care*. Oxford: Blackwell.

Maher, P. and Best, R. 1985: 'Preparation and Support for Pastoral Care – A Survey of Current Provision'. In Lang, P. and Marland, M. (eds), *New Directions in Pastoral Care*. Oxford: Blackwell.

Marland, M. 1974: *Pastoral Care*. London: Heinemann.

Marland, M. 1985: 'Parents, Schooling and the Welfare of Pupils'. In Ribbins, P. (ed), *Schooling and Welfare*. Lewes: Falmer.

Merton, R. 1949: *Social Theory and Social Structure*. Glencoe: The Free Press.

McIntyre, D. and Brown, S. 1978: 'The Conceptualisation of Attainment'. *British Educational Research Journal* Vol 4, No 2.

McLeod, J. 1983: 'Learning Disability is for Educators'. *Journal of Learning Disabilities* Vol 16, No 1, January.

McNicholas, J. 1979: 'Aims of Remedial Education – A Critique'. In Gains, C. and McNicholas, J. (eds), *Remedial Education: Guidelines for the Future*. London: Longman.

Moore, B. 1970: *Guidance in Comprehensive Schools*. Slough: NFER

Moseley, D. 1975: *Special Provision for Reading*. Slough: NFER

Murgatroyd, S. (ed) 1980: *Helping the Troubled Child*. London: Harper and Row.

Nicholls, A. 1979: *The Planning and Implementation of an Educational Innovation: A Case Study*. Unpublished PhD thesis. Queens University, Belfast.

Nicholls, A. 1983: *Managing Educational Innovations*. London: Allen and Unwin.

Oskamp, S. 1965: 'Overconfidence in Case-study Judgements'. *Journal of Consulting Psychology* Vol 29.

Parlett, M. and Hamilton, D. 1972: *Evaluation as Illumination*. Edinburgh: Edinburgh University Press.

Peeke, G. 1984: 'Teachers and Curriculum Change'. *The NATFHE Journal* Vol 9, No 3, April.

Pikulski, J. 1975: 'Assessing Information about Intelligence and Reading', *Reading Teacher* Vol 29.

Pritchard, D. 1963: *Education and the Handicapped: 1760–1960*. London: Routledge and Kegan Paul.

Postman, N. and Weingartner, C. 1971: *Teaching as a Subversive Activity*. Harmondsworth: Penguin.

Quicke, J. 1981: 'Special Educational Needs and the Comprehensive Principle: Some Implications of Ideological Critique'. *Remedial Education* Vol 16, No 2, May.

Raddon, R. 1984: *Planning Learning Resource Centres in Schools and Colleges*. Aldershot: Gower.

Raybould, E., Roberts, B. and Wedell, K. 1980: *Helping the Low Achiever in the Secondary School*. Educational Review Occasional Publication No 7.

Ribbins, P. (ed) 1985: *Schooling and Welfare*. Lewes: Falmer.

Ribbins, P. and Best, R. 1985: 'Pastoral Care: Theory, Practice and the Growth of Research'. In Lang, P. and Marland, M. (eds), *New Directions in Pastoral Care*. Oxford: Blackwell.

Ribbins, P., Best, R. and Jarvis, C. 1982: *Teacher Attitudes to Pastoral Care*. Unpublished research report.

Richardson, E. 1973: *The Teacher, the School, and the Task of Management*. London: Heinemann.

Rogers, C. 1967: *On Becoming a Person*. London: Constable.

Rosenthal, R. and Jacobson, L. 1968: *Pygmalion in the Classroom: Teacher Expectations and Pupils' Intellectual Development*. New York: Holt, Rinehart and Winston.

Rowe, A. 1971: *School as a Guidance Community*. St. Albans: Hart-Davis Educational.

Rutter, M., Maughan, B., Mortimore, P. and Ouston, J. 1979: *Fifteen Thousands hours*. Somerset: Open Books.

Sampson, O. 1975: *Remedial Education*. London: Routledge and Kegan Paul.

Sampson, O. and Pumfrey, P. 1970: 'A Study of Remedial Education in the Secondary Stage of Schooling'. *Remedial Education* Vol 5, No 3, October.

Schonell, F. 1942: *Backwardness in the Basic Subjects*. Edinburgh: Oliver and Boyd.

Stenhouse, L. 1975: *An Introduction to Curriculum Research and Development*. London: Heinemann.

Simon, B. 1960: *Studies in the History of Education, 1780–1870*. London: Lawrence & Wishart.

Tabberer, R. and Allman, J. 1983: *Introducing Study Skills*. Windsor: NFER-Nelson.

Toffler, A. 1970: *Future Shock*. London: Bodley Head.

Tomlinson, S. 1982: *A Sociology of Special Education*. London: Routledge and Kegan Paul.

Tough, J. 1976: *Listening to Children Talking*. Glasgow: Ward Lock Educational.

Valentine, C. 1968: *Culture and Poverty*. London: Chicago University Press.

Warner, F. 1890: *Lectures on Mental Faculty*. See Burt, F. (1952).

Welton, J. 1982: 'Schools in the Welfare Network'. *Child Care. Health and Development*, No 8.

Welton, J. 1985: 'Schools and a Multi-professional Approach to Welfare'. In Ribbins P. (ed), *Schooling and Welfare*. Lewes: Falmer.

Westwood, P. 1975: *The Remedial Teachers Handbook*. Edinburgh: Oliver and Boyd.

Widlake, P. 1975: 'Remedial Education at the Crossroads'. *Remedial Education* Vol 10, No 3.

Widlake, P. (ed) 1977: *Remedial Education: Programmes and Progress*. London: Longman.

Williams, A. 1970: *Basic Subjects for Slower learners*. London: Methuen.

Williamson, D. 1980: 'Pastoral Care or Pastoralisation?'. In Best, R. et al (eds, *Perspectives on Pastoral Care*. London: Heinemann.

Wright, C. 1965: *An English Word Count*. Pretoria: National Bureau of Educational and Social Research.

Young, M. (ed) 1971: *Knowledge and Control*. London: Collier-MacMillan.

Index